EFFECTIVE MANAGEMENT SKILLS

FOR TECHNICAL PROFESSIONS

I0466856

PRANAB KUMAR DAS GUPTA

KINDLE DIRECT PUBLISHING

Price: $ 14.99

Disclaimer: The information provided in this book is intended for general informational purposes only. The opinions expressed herein belong to the author and do not necessarily represent the official stance of any individual, agency, organization, employer, or company. Although the author and publisher have taken great care to ensure the accuracy and comprehensiveness of the information in this book, they do not accept responsibility for any errors, inaccuracies, omissions, or inconsistencies contained within. Any reliance on the information presented is entirely at your own risk. The author and publisher disclaim any liability for any loss or damage (including indirect or consequential loss) that may arise directly or indirectly from the use of, or reliance on, the content in this book. Mentions of specific commercial products, processes, or services using trade names, trademarks, manufacturers, or otherwise do not indicate endorsement, recommendation, or preference by the author or publisher. This book does not serve as a substitute for professional advice across legal, medical, financial, or any other fields. Readers are advised to seek appropriate professional assistance tailored to their individual circumstances.

DEDICATION

This book is dedicated to Lord Krishna, who has imparted timeless wisdom on management and the art of leading a balanced and fulfilling life through His divine discourse, the Bhagavad Gita. His teachings continue to guide and inspire mankind towards excellence and inner peace.

TABLE OF CONTENT

PREFACE

Younger and mid-career professionals often struggle with evolving technologies and management skills, resulting in increased stress and potential layoffs. Ineffective management practices and resistance to change exacerbate these issues, particularly since senior roles demand strong management competence.

This book is ideal for younger and mid-career professionals who plan to work well into their 60s and beyond. It provides valuable insights into modern day management practices and techniques for sustaining a long and fulfilling career. If you are dedicated to a long-term professional journey, this book offers the guidance you need to navigate and thrive in the evolving workplace, ensuring that you remain engaged and productive throughout your extended career. It's specifically designed for those committed to a prolonged work life and the unique challenges and opportunities that come with it.

This book is also useful for those who plan to pursue an MBA after graduation as well. It is meant to provide them with the knowledge and skills that are on par with those of students who are starting an MBA program with a bachelor's degree in management or two to three years of work experience.

Most of the professionals and students lack confidence in the field of management. This book aims to enhance their knowledge by providing a thorough yet succinct formal education in management. It acts as a valuable tool for rapidly acquiring theoretical knowledge, complementing, and improving their overall management skills. The 200+ questions in the book will help build confidence.

Time is valuable, and it is usually impractical for working professionals to read for extended periods. This book is structured to accelerate your learning curve effectively. Each chapter suggests starting with a set of questions designed to assess your existing knowledge. If you can answer all the questions correctly, you may skip the chapter or quickly scan its contents. However, if you find that you cannot answer majority of the questions, it is recommended that you read the chapter thoroughly at your own pace. After completing the chapter, revisit the questions to reinforce and deepen your understanding.

This book is structured into two parts to facilitate both personal growth and organizational effectiveness. **Part 1: Personal and Professional Development** covers essential topics such as **Overcoming Procrastination, Time Management, Stress Management,** and **Depression Management,** providing strategies to enhance individual productivity and well-being. It also addresses **Presentation Skills, Situational Awareness,** and **Communication Proficiency** to improve interpersonal effectiveness. Further, it explores maintaining **Motivation at Workplace,** employing **Six Thinking Hats** for problem-solving, and **Creativity and it's Blocks** while being innovative and identifying blocks to creativity.

Part 2: Organizational Management focuses on optimizing team and organizational performance. It includes strategies for **Conflict Management,** understanding **Team Dynamics,** and utilizing **Transactional Analysis** and **Johari's Window** for better interpersonal relations. The part further delves into **Competency Mapping,** effective **Leading and Managing,** and explores motivational theories like **Theory X and Theory Y.** It also covers **Polarity Management** for balancing competing values, **Decision Making and Problem Solving** for strategic success, transitioning from **Effectiveness to Excellence,** and assessing the **Return on Training Investment** to ensure valuable developmental outcomes. This book aims to equip readers with comprehensive tools for achieving personal excellence and organizational success.

This book covers the management topics necessary for effectively managing oneself and others in real-world situations. All chapters are concise, self-contained, and clear, allowing them to be read in any order without losing continuity. Case studies and examples provided in each chapter serve as excellent resources for grasping theoretical concepts, and to enhance the reading experience.

The main goal of the book is to spark interest in management, encouraging you to delve deeper and master the subject.

Happy learning.

Pranab Kumar Das Gupta

ACKNOWLEDGMENTS

I am deeply grateful for the invaluable contributions of all those who have played a crucial role in bringing this book to life.

First of all, I express sincere gratitude to my family members and siblings for their encouragement and faith in my abilities.

I extend my appreciation to the spiritual group whose unwavering dedication and inspiration have been a guiding light throughout this journey. Special thanks to Mr. Arindam Pathak, Ms. Surekha Bharne, Dr. Maya C. Sahajwalla, Ms Prabha Sridhar, Ms. Kalpana Manoj Parihar, Ms. Saloni Raizada, Ms. Rita Verman Maheshwari, Mr. Shrikrishna Verman, Mr. Priyesh Doshi and Mr. Madhusudhan Mendu R for their wisdom and support, which have nurtured the development of this book.

I am thankful to my superiors, Dr. Samir V. Kamat, Dr. BK Das, Prof. Prateek Kishore and Mr. SK Nayak, for their professional support and understanding, enabling me to dedicate time to this literary pursuit.

To my dear friends Mr. Ram Prosad Mondal, Mr. Pradip Duttagupta, Dr. HS Panda, Dr. S Padhy, Col Ramchandra Kshetri, and Col. Satish Kumar: Your support has been crucial in motivating me to share my thoughts with the world. I also want to thank Mahesh for his meticulous attention to detail, ensuring that this book reads well and looks great. Thanks to Dipankar, Asit, Somanath, and Rabinarayan for their timely help with this book.

I express my deep gratitude to the pioneers of management techniques, tools, and concepts that have significantly enhanced our ability to manage tasks efficiently and successfully.

I cherish the memories of my parents, Dr. AB Das Gupta and Ms. Anjali Das Gupta, along with my eldest sister, Ms. Kalpana Choudhury.

Lastly, in deep reverence, I bow to Lord Krishna, Lord Shiva, Surya Dev, and Bajrangbali. I seek their divine blessings and guidance as I walk the righteous path of dharma.

Pranab Kumar Das Gupta

PART 1

PERSONAL

AND

PROFESSIONAL DEVELOPMENT

CHAPTER 1

OVERCOMING PROCRASTINATION

INTRODUCTION

Procrastination, the act of delaying or postponing tasks, is a commonly faced challenge that can impede productivity and lead to stress. While breaking the habit of procrastination may seem daunting, it can be successfully managed with a combination of effective strategies and a positive mind-set.

Kindly answer all the questions given at the end of the chapter. This will help you evaluate your understanding of the topic and decide whether you need a quick review or a more detailed study.

UNDERSTANDING PROCRASTINATION

To effectively address procrastination, it is crucial to delve into its underlying causes. Procrastination often arises from various factors such as the fear of failure, perfectionism, lack of motivation, or overwhelming tasks. Identifying and acknowledging these root causes is essential for combating procrastination successfully.

Break Tasks into Smaller Steps

A practical approach to tackling procrastination is breaking down large tasks into smaller, more manageable steps. By dividing tasks into achievable increments, the feeling of being overwhelmed is minimized, making it easier to initiate the work.

Example: Consider Prabha, who faced a monumental task of writing a 20-page research paper for her history class. Overwhelmed, she procrastinated for weeks until she decided to divide the project into smaller tasks like selecting a topic, conducting research, outlining, writing sections, and revising. By focusing on each step individually, Prabha found it easier to make progress and completed her paper ahead of schedule.

Establish Clear Goals and Deadlines

Creating clear and attainable goals, coupled with specific deadlines, provides structure and motivation for tasks. Well-defined deadlines generate a sense of urgency, making it harder to justify delaying completion.

Example: Mahesh was struggling to finish a project at work due to the absence of specific deadlines for each phase. Following his manager's advice, he outlined a timeline with milestones for research, initial drafts, and final revisions. This structured roadmap enabled Mahesh to stay on course and successfully complete the project on time.

Implement the Pomodoro Technique

Embracing the Pomodoro Technique involves working for fixed intervals, typically 25 minutes, followed by short breaks. This method enhances concentration and reduces the inclination to procrastinate by establishing a balanced work-rest pattern.

Example: Kalpana, a freelance writer prone to distractions like social media, adopted the Pomodoro Technique. Setting a timer for 25 minutes, she dedicated herself to writing and then took a 5-minute break. This structured approach significantly improved her focus and productivity.

Minimize Distractions

Identifying and eliminating distractions is crucial in combatting procrastination. Removing distractions helps in maintaining focus on the task at hand.

Example: Dipankar, a student, recognized that frequent phone notifications hindered his study sessions. To mitigate this, he activated airplane mode on his phone and opted for a quiet study environment in the library. By reducing distractions, Dipankar enhanced his concentration and completed assignments more efficiently.

Prioritize Tasks

By prioritizing tasks based on their urgency and importance, procrastination can be discouraged, ensuring that crucial tasks are tackled promptly.

Example: Consider Anna, faced with multiple projects and varied deadlines. She created a priority list, organizing tasks based on urgency and significance.

By attending to the most critical tasks first, Anna effectively managed her workload, avoiding last-minute rushes.

Embrace Accountability

Sharing goals with someone else fosters accountability, decreasing the likelihood of procrastination.

Example: Tom and his friend Jerry, preparing for a competitive exam, became study partners to hold each other accountable. Setting weekly goals and regular progress checks enabled them to stay on track and achieve their study objectives.

Reward Progress

Implementing a reward system provides motivation to accomplish tasks. Knowing a reward wait upon task completion can make the process more enticing and fulfilling.

Example: Radha, a graphic designer, struggling with project delays, introduced a reward system. After completing a significant task, she treated herself to a favorite snack or short walk. These small incentives kept her motivated and made her work more enjoyable.

OVERCOMING COMMON OBSTACLES

Addressing common obstacles like perfectionism, fear of failure, and lack of motivation is vital in managing procrastination effectively:

Perfectionism: Recognize that perfection is unattainable and that progress is more significant than perfection.

Fear of Failure: View mistakes as opportunities for learning and growth.

Lack of Motivation: Find personal significance in tasks and acknowledge the benefits of completing them.

Example: Ram, an aspiring author, overcame procrastination in writing his novel by shifting his focus from perfection to enjoyment. By adopting a mindset centered on writing for pleasure, he cultivated consistency and steadily improved his writing skills.

CASE STUDY: OVERCOMING PROCRASTINATION IN THE WORKPLACE

Background

ABC Corporation, a mid-sized tech company, noticed a decline in employee productivity and an increase in project delays. Upon investigation, the HR department identified procrastination as a significant factor contributing to these issues. To address this, the company implemented a structured approach to address procrastination, drawing on strategies and techniques known to be effective.

Problem Statement

Employees at ABC Corporation were frequently delaying tasks, resulting in missed deadlines, increased stress, and lower overall productivity. Key issues included fear of failure, perfectionism, lack of motivation, and overwhelming tasks.

Implementation Plan

Understanding Procrastination: A series of workshops were conducted to educate employees about the causes and effects of procrastination. Employees were encouraged to identify their personal triggers for procrastination.

Break Tasks into Smaller Steps: Employees were trained to break down large projects into smaller, manageable tasks. Tools like task lists and project management software were introduced to help with task segmentation.

Establish Clear Goals and Deadlines: Teams set clear, attainable goals for each phase of their projects. Specific deadlines were assigned to each task, creating a sense of urgency and structure.

Implement the Pomodoro Technique: Employees were introduced to the Pomodoro Technique, working in 25-minute intervals followed by short breaks. This method was adopted across various departments to enhance focus and productivity.

Minimize Distractions: Distraction-free workspaces were created, and policies were implemented to limit interruptions. Employees were encouraged to use tools like Do Not Disturb modes on their devices during work intervals.

Prioritize Tasks: Training sessions on prioritization techniques, such as the Eisenhower Matrix, were held. Employees learned to categorize tasks by urgency and importance, ensuring that critical tasks were addressed promptly.

Embrace Accountability: A buddy system was introduced, where employees paired up to share goals and hold each other accountable. Regular check-ins and progress reviews were scheduled to maintain accountability.

Reward Progress: A reward system was established, providing incentives for meeting deadlines and achieving milestones. Rewards ranged from small treats to extra break time and recognition in team meetings.

Outcomes

Increased Productivity: Employee productivity improved significantly, with projects being completed on or ahead of schedule.

Reduced Stress: Clear goals and deadlines, along with structured work intervals, reduced employee stress levels.

Enhanced Focus: The Pomodoro Technique and minimized distractions led to better concentration and higher quality work.

Improved Accountability: The buddy system and regular check-ins developed a culture of accountability and support.

Higher Job Satisfaction: Employees reported higher job satisfaction due to the effective strategies and rewards system.

ABC Corporation's implementation of procrastination management strategies based on breaking tasks into smaller steps, setting clear goals, using the Pomodoro Technique, minimizing distractions, prioritizing tasks, setting accountability, and rewarding progress proved successful. The case study highlights the effectiveness of these strategies in overcoming procrastination, leading to improved productivity, reduced stress, and higher job satisfaction. This structured approach can serve as a model for other organizations facing similar challenges. By understanding the root causes of procrastination and adopting practical strategies, companies can enhance their workforce's productivity and well-being.

CONCLUSION

While procrastination poses a common challenge, implementing effective strategies can help manage it efficiently. By incorporating techniques such as breaking tasks into smaller steps, setting clear goals, utilizing methods like the Pomodoro Technique, eliminating distractions, prioritizing tasks, embracing accountability, and rewarding progress, individuals can conquer procrastination and enhance their productivity. Remember, commencing with modest steps, maintaining consistency, and practicing self-compassion during the journey toward your goals are key aspects to success.

-------------- **Multiple Choice Type Questions** --------------

Q1. What is a commonly faced challenge that can impede productivity and lead to stress?

A. Overconfidence
B. Procrastination
C. Perfectionism
D. Multitasking

Q2. Which of the following is NOT a cause of procrastination?

A. Fear of failure
B. Perfectionism
C. Overconfidence
D. Lack of motivation

Q3. What is the first strategy mentioned for overcoming procrastination?

A. Establishing clear goals and deadlines
B. Breaking tasks into smaller steps
C. Implementing the Pomodoro Technique
D. Embracing accountability

Q4. What is the purpose of the Pomodoro Technique?

A. To break tasks into smaller steps
B. To establish clear goals and deadlines
C. To enhance concentration and reduce procrastination
D. To create a reward system for task completion

Q5. Which strategy involves organizing tasks based on urgency and significance?

    A. Breaking tasks into smaller steps

    B. Prioritizing tasks

    C. Minimizing distractions

    D. Embracing accountability

-------------------- **Match The Following** --------------------

Q1. Match the obstacle with the corresponding approach to overcome it:

1. Perfectionism	A. View mistakes as opportunities for learning and growth.
2. Fear of Failure	B. Find personal significance in tasks and acknowledge the benefits of completing them.
3. Lack of Motivation	C. Recognize that perfection is unattainable and that progress is more significant.

CHAPTER 2

TIME MANAGEMENT

INTRODUCTION

Time management plays a vital role in all areas of our lives, impacting personal relationships as well as professional achievements. It involves the careful planning, organization, and control of the time allocated to different activities. Effective time management enables individuals to achieve more in less time, reduce stress levels, and pave the way for career advancement. This chapter explores the fundamentals, tactics, and methods of time management, offering practical guidance to help you optimize your time utilization.

Ensure that you exert effort to answer all the questions provided in the chapter. This method will assist you in assessing your comprehension of the subject and determining whether a brief review or a more thorough study is necessary.

UNDERSTANDING TIME MANAGEMENT

The Significance of Time

Time is a limited resource that cannot be saved or stockpiled for later use, unlike money or possessions. Each day consists of only 24 hours, and how you utilize these hours determines your productivity and success. Poor time management can result in missed deadlines, heightened stress, and diminished work quality. On the other hand, mastering time management can enhance efficiency, increase productivity, and provide more time for personal pursuits.

The Pareto Principle

A cornerstone concept in time management is the Pareto Principle, commonly known as the 80/20 Rule. This principle suggests that 80% of outcomes stem from 20% of efforts. Understanding and applying this principle can help identify and concentrate on tasks that yield the most significant results. By

	Urgent	Not Urgent
Important	Activities Crisis Deadlines	Activities Prevention Planning
Not Important	Activities Interruption Phone Calls	Activities Time Waits Pleasantries

Figure 1 [Eisenhower Matrix]

focusing on these high-impact activities, you can achieve notable outcomes with minimal effort.

STRATEGIES FOR EFFECTIVE TIME MANAGEMENT

Setting Objectives

The initial step in effective time management is establishing clear and attainable goals. Goals offer direction and purpose, assisting you in concentrating on what truly matters. These goals should be Specific, Measurable, Achievable, Relevant, and Time-bound (SMART). For example, rather than setting a vague goal such as "get fit," a SMART goal would be "exercise for 30 minutes, five days a week."

Prioritizing Tasks

Not all tasks carry equal weight. Prioritization involves identifying the most crucial tasks and addressing them first. An effective method for prioritizing tasks is the Eisenhower Matrix, which categorizes tasks into four quadrants based on urgency and importance (Figure 1).

Urgent and Important: Tasks requiring immediate attention.

Important but Not Urgent: Tasks crucial but can be deferred.

Urgent but Not Important: Tasks demanding urgency but can be delegated.

Not Urgent and Not Important: Tasks neither urgent nor important and can be potentially eliminated.

By focusing on the first two quadrants, you ensure that your time is devoted to activities aligning with your objectives and values.

DEVELOPING A SCHEDULE

A well-organized schedule is essential for effective time management. Utilize tools like calendars, planners, or digital apps to structure your day, week, and month. Divide your schedule into time blocks allocated for specific tasks. Include breaks and leisure activities to prevent burnout. Regularly review and adjust your schedule to ensure it remains realistic and aligned with your goals.

OVERCOMING PROCRASTINATION

Procrastination poses a significant challenge to time management. It involves delaying or postponing tasks, often resulting in rushed and subpar work. To combat procrastination, break tasks into smaller segments, set deadlines, and reward yourself upon completion. Techniques like the Pomodoro Technique can assist in maintaining focus and productivity by alternating work periods with short breaks.

TECHNIQUES FOR IMPROVING PRODUCTIVITY

Time Blocking

Time blocking entails dedicating specific time blocks to different tasks or activities, creating a regimented routine that minimizes distractions and enhances focus. For example, you may allocate mornings to high-priority tasks, reserve afternoons for meetings, and designate evenings for personal pursuits.

The Two-Minute Rule

Popularized by productivity expert David Allen, the Two-Minute Rule suggests that tasks requiring less than two minutes for completion should be tackled immediately. This rule prevents small tasks from accumulating and overwhelming your to-do list.

Batch Processing

Batch processing involves grouping similar tasks together and completing them in a single session. For instance, instead of checking emails sporadically, set specific times to handle all emails at once. This technique reduces context switching and boosts efficiency.

Delegation

Delegation is crucial for effective time management, involving the assignment of tasks to others to free up time for more critical activities. Identify tasks suitable for delegation, select the appropriate individuals, provide clear instructions, and follow up to ensure successful task completion.

MAINTAINING WORK-LIFE BALANCE

Establishing Boundaries

An essential aspect of time management is maintaining a healthy work-life balance. Set clear boundaries between work and personal time, refraining from engaging in work-related activities outside of designated hours. Communicate these boundaries to colleagues and family members to ensure that your personal time is respected.

Importance of Taking Breaks

Regular breaks play a vital role in enhancing productivity and preventing burnout. Incorporating short breaks throughout the workday can rejuvenate your mind and enhance concentration. Moreover, indulging in longer breaks, such as vacations, enables you to recharge and come back to work with revitalized energy.

Embracing Self-Care

Make self-care a priority by engaging in activities like exercise, pursuing hobbies, and spending quality time with loved ones. These practices are effective in reducing stress, enhancing mental well-being, and overall quality of life. By nurturing yourself, you equip yourself with the vigor and focus necessary for effective time management.

UTILIZING TOOLS AND RESOURCES

Digital Assistance

Numerous digital tools are available to support time management:

Calendars: Platforms like Google Calendar or Microsoft Outlook are useful for scheduling and organizing tasks.

To-Do Lists: Applications such as Todoist or Microsoft To Do aid in task tracking and prioritization.

Time Trackers: Utilize tools like Toggl or Clockify to monitor time usage, offering insights for improvement.

Physical Aids

Traditional tools like planners, notebooks, and whiteboards can also be valuable for managing time. Jotting down tasks and schedules can boost memory retention and serve as a visual cue for your commitments.

OVERCOMING COMMON HURDLES

Tackling Distractions

Distractions pose a significant challenge to effective time management. Identify common distractions, like social media, and employ strategies to minimize their impact. This may involve scheduling specific times for social media use, utilizing website blockers, or creating a distraction-free workspace.

Addressing Overwhelm

Feeling overwhelmed by tasks and obligations is common. Combat this by breaking tasks into smaller segments, prioritizing effectively, and utilizing techniques like time blocking. Remember to delegate when feasible and seek assistance from colleagues, friends, or family.

Sustaining Motivation

Sustaining motivation, particularly for long-term goals, can be demanding. Keep your objectives visible and celebrate incremental victories. Maintain motivation by focusing on the benefits of task completion and the gratification of achieving your goals.

CASE STUDY: ENHANCING TIME MGT PRACTICES AT ABC CORPORATION

Context

ABC Corporation, a rapidly expanding technology firm, faced challenges with decreased productivity and heightened employee stress levels. Acknowledging the importance of efficient time management, the leadership aimed to boost productivity, alleviate stress, and promote a healthier work-life balance.

Implementation

In response, the company rolled out a comprehensive time management training program. This training underlined the value of time, introduced the Pareto Principle, and elucidated diverse strategies for optimizing time management. Employees received instruction on setting SMART goals, utilizing the Eisenhower Matrix for task prioritization, and crafting organized schedules.

Goal Setting

Staff members were urged to establish specific, measurable, achievable, relevant, and time-bound (SMART) goals. For example, shifting from a vague objective like "enhance coding skills" to a SMART goal like "successfully complete an advanced Python course within three months."

Task Prioritization

The Eisenhower Matrix was employed to categorize tasks according to urgency and importance. Employees learned to tackle urgent and important responsibilities first, such as client deliverables and crucial project milestones, prior to addressing important but not urgent tasks like skill enhancement and strategic planning.

Schedule Development

Employees leveraged digital solutions like Google Calendar and Todoist to structure their schedules. By implementing time blocking, specific time slots were allocated for high-priority tasks, meetings, and personal activities. Regular reviews ensured that schedules remained achievable and in alignment with goals.

Overcoming Procrastination

To combat procrastination, employees were introduced to the Pomodoro Technique. This technique involved 25-minute focused work intervals followed by brief breaks. Tasks were subdivided into smaller, manageable segments, each with set deadlines. Employees were encouraged to reward themselves upon the completion of tasks.

Boosting Productivity

The adoption of batch processing enabled employees to group and complete similar tasks in one session, minimizing context switching. Additionally, the Two-Minute Rule was implemented to address quick tasks promptly, averting task accumulation. Delegation was also encouraged, with tasks assigned to team members along with clear instructions and follow-ups.

Work-Life Balance Maintenance

Clear boundaries were established between work and personal time to prevent work-related activities outside designated hours. These boundaries were communicated to colleagues and family members. Moreover, regular breaks and vacations were promoted to prevent burnout and uphold productivity levels.

Tool Utilization

Digital tools like Toggl and Clockify facilitated time tracking, offering insights into time allocation. Physical aids such as planners and whiteboards aided employees in visually organizing their tasks and schedules.

Addressing Challenges

Strategies were implemented to combat distractions, including the use of website blockers and the creation of distraction-free work environments. Employees were trained to manage feelings of overwhelm by breaking tasks into smaller segments and prioritizing effectively. Sustaining motivation was achieved through celebrating incremental victories and emphasizing the benefits of task completion.

Results

The structured approach to time management led to a significant improvement in productivity and a notable decrease in stress levels at ABC Corporation. Employees reported enhanced work-life balance and increased job satisfaction. The company observed a 25% enhancement in project completion rates and a 15% reduction in employee burnout. This case study demonstrates the transformative influence of effective time management strategies on organizational performance and employee well-being.

CONCLUSION

Effective time management is a critical skill that significantly influences both personal and professional aspects of life. By establishing clear goals, prioritizing tasks, structuring schedules, and employing diverse productivity strategies, you can optimize your time utilization. Remember to uphold a healthy work-life balance, prioritize self-care, and utilize the available tools and resources. Effective time management results in heightened productivity, diminished stress, and a more gratifying life.

-------------- Multiple Choice Type Questions --------------

Q1. What is the initial step in effective time management?

    A. Developing a schedule

    B. Setting objectives

    C. Overcoming procrastination

    D. Embracing self-care

Q2. Which principle suggests that 80% of outcomes stem from 20% of efforts?

A. Eisenhower Matrix
B. Time Blocking
C. Pareto Principle
D. Two-Minute Rule

Q3. Which technique involves dedicating specific time blocks to different tasks?

A. Delegation
B. Batch Processing
C. Time Blocking
D. Two-Minute Rule

Q4. What should SMART goals be?

A. Simple, Measurable, Active, Relevant, Time-bound
B. Specific, Measurable, Achievable, Relevant, Time-bound
C. Specific, Measurable, Active, Realistic, Time-bound
D. Simple, Motivational, Achievable, Realistic, Time-bound

Q5. What does the Eisenhower Matrix categorize tasks based on?

A. Importance and difficulty
B. Urgency and importance
C. Time required and complexity
D. Importance and resources needed

Q6. What method involves tackling tasks requiring less than two minutes immediately?

A. Time Blocking
B. Two-Minute Rule
C. Batch Processing
D. Delegation

Q7. Which tools are used for scheduling and organizing tasks digitally?

   A. Notebooks and planners

   B. Whiteboards and sticky notes

   C. Google Calendar and Microsoft Outlook

   D. Digital timers and alarms

Q8. What is crucial for maintaining a healthy work-life balance?

   A. Setting clear boundaries between work and personal time

   B. Working overtime regularly

   C. Combining work and personal tasks

   D. Ignoring personal commitments for work

Q9. Which productivity technique involves grouping similar tasks together?

   A. Delegation

   B. Two-Minute Rule

   C. Time Blocking

   D. Batch Processing

Q10. What should you do to combat procrastination?

   A. Set vague goals

   B. Delay tasks until the last minute

   C. Break tasks into smaller segments and set deadlines

   D. Ignore deadlines and work randomly

-------------------- Match The Following --------------------

Q1. Match the following concept in Time Management with their descriptions:

1. The Pareto Principle	A. SMART goals
2. Prioritizing Tasks	B. 80/20 Rule
3. Setting Objectives	C. Identifying distractions
4. Tackling Distractions	D. Break tasks into smaller segments
5. Addressing Overwhelm	E. Eisenhower Matrix

CHAPTER 3

STRESS MANAGEMENT

INTRODUCTION

Stress management requires utilizing various techniques and strategies to regulate an individual's stress levels, particularly chronic stress, with the aim of enhancing daily functioning. Successful stress management promotes a well-rounded life, betters mental and physical well-being, and boosts productivity. Key methods include engaging in physical activity, practicing relaxation techniques, effective time management, and seeking social support. By identifying stress triggers and coping mechanisms, individuals can prevent stress from becoming overwhelming. Consistently implementing these strategies can assist individuals in maintaining a composed and focused approach when facing life's challenges.

Please answer all the questions given at the end of the chapter. This will help you evaluate your understanding of the topic and decide whether you need a quick review or a more detailed study.

SOURCES OF STRESS

Workplace stress is a prevalent issue affecting numerous employees across different positions and industries. Several factors contribute to stress in the workplace:

Workload

One of the primary sources of stress is having an excessive amount of work within a limited timeframe. Employees often feel overwhelmed when facing unrealistic deadlines or a high workload.

Job Security

Concerns about job stability can be a significant stressor. During uncertain economic periods or organizational restructuring, employees may fear for their job security.

Work-Life Balance

Balancing work and personal life can be challenging. When work responsibilities seep into personal time, it can lead to stress, particularly for individuals with family obligations or other commitments outside of work.

Interpersonal Relationships

Relationships with colleagues, supervisors, and clients can also contribute to stress. Conflict, lack of support, or poor communication can create a stressful work environment.

Role Ambiguity

Unclear job expectations can induce stress. When employees are unsure about their responsibilities or performance evaluation criteria, it can lead to anxiety and frustration.

Environmental Factors

The physical work environment can also play a role in stress levels. Factors such as noise, limited privacy, inadequate lighting, and uncomfortable working conditions can impact an employee's stress levels.

IMPACT OF STRESS

Stress can profoundly influence an employee's performance, manifesting in the following ways:

Decreased Productivity

High stress levels often result in reduced productivity. Stressed employees may struggle to concentrate, make decisions, and stay focused, leading to lower output and increased errors.

Poor Quality of Work

Stress can compromise the quality of work. Stressed employees may rush through tasks, overlook details, or make mistakes, affecting the overall quality of products or services.

Increased Absenteeism

Stress can contribute to physical and mental health issues like headaches, fatigue, anxiety, and depression. Consequently, stressed employees may take more sick days, disrupting workflow and reducing overall productivity.

Lower Morale

A stressful work environment can diminish employee morale. Constant stress may leave employees feeling unmotivated, disengaged, and less committed to their work, potentially increasing turnover rates and recruitment costs.

Strained Relationships

Stress can strain relationships with colleagues and supervisors. Stressed employees may exhibit irritability, impatience, or reduced cooperation, leading to conflicts and hindered teamwork.

STRESS MANAGEMENT STRATEGIES

Managing stress is vital for well-being and optimal work performance. Here are some effective stress management techniques.

Time Management

Efficient time management enables employees to prioritize tasks, set realistic deadlines, and incorporate breaks. Tools like to-do lists and calendars aid in organizing workload efficiently.

Relaxation Techniques

Practices such as deep breathing, meditation, and muscle relaxation can alleviate stress, promoting relaxation and mental well-being.

Physical Activity

Regular exercise is a potent stress reliever, releasing endorphins that elevate mood. Encouraging physical activities like walks or stretching can reduce stress levels.

Healthy Lifestyle Choices

Maintaining a balanced diet, ample sleep, and limiting caffeine and alcohol intake contribute to stress management.

Seeking Support

Openly discussing stress with colleagues, supervisors, friends, or family members can be beneficial. Professional services like counseling provide additional support.

Creating a Positive Work Environment

Employers can aid in stress reduction by setting clear job expectations, offering professional development opportunities, recognizing achievements, and promoting open communication.

Setting Boundaries

Establishing boundaries between work and personal life is critical for stress management. Disengaging from work during non-working hours promotes relaxation and rejuvenation.

Mindfulness and Meditation

Practicing mindfulness and meditation aids in maintaining focus and tranquility, reducing stress and enhancing well-being.

Stress Management Training

Providing stress management training equips employees with tools to handle stress effectively, covering topics like resiliency and coping strategies.

Flexible Work Arrangements

Offering flexible work options can support work-life balance, diminishing stress levels.

CASE STUDY: STRESS MANAGEMENT IN A CORPORATE ENVIRONMENT

Context

TechSolutions Inc., a rapidly growing technology firm, has undergone substantial expansion in recent years. The company's workforce has reported escalating stress levels, affecting productivity, increasing absenteeism, and straining team dynamics. To address these issues, the HR department initiated a comprehensive stress management program.

Scenario

Swati, a project manager at TechSolutions, is grappling with significant stress due to her heavy workload, unclear job expectations, and challenges in balancing work and personal life. Her productivity has declined, and she often feels overwhelmed and exhausted. Swati's stress has also impacted her relationships at work, leading to irritability and reduced cooperation.

Sources of Stress

Workload: Managing multiple critical projects with tight deadlines leaves Swati feeling overwhelmed and hampers task completion efficiency.

Outcome: Reduced productivity and work quality due to rushed tasks and errors.

Job Security: Recent company reorganization has raised concerns about Swati's job stability, adding to her stress.

Outcome: Increased anxiety and difficulty focusing on tasks.

Work-Life Balance: Struggling to juggle work and personal commitments, Swati often works late and misses' family events.

Outcome: Heightened stress and burnout resulting in increased absenteeism.

Interpersonal Relationships: Conflicts with a colleague and inadequate support from her supervisor contribute to Swati's stress.

Outcome: Strained relationships and diminished team cooperation.

Role Ambiguity: Uncertainty about her responsibilities and performance evaluation causes anxiety and frustration.

Outcome: Lower morale and disengagement.

Environmental Factors: Swati's noisy and lacking privacy workspace hinders focus and adds to her stress.

Outcome: Increased stress and decreased productivity.

Impact of Stress

Decreased Productivity: Difficulty concentrating and staying focused have led to lower output and increased errors.

Poor Quality of Work: Rushed tasks and oversight of details compromise work quality.

Increased Absenteeism: Stress-related health issues like headaches and fatigue result in more sick days.

Lower Morale: Unmotivated and disengaged feelings affect work commitment.

Strained Relationships: Irritability and impatience strain relationships, hindering teamwork.

Stress Management Strategies

Time Management: Utilizing to-do lists and calendars to prioritize tasks and set realistic deadlines.

Outcome: Improved organization and reduced overwhelm.

Relaxation Techniques: Engaging in deep breathing exercises and meditation during breaks to alleviate stress.

Outcome: Improved mental well-being and reduced anxiety.

Physical Activity: Incorporating regular exercise like walking and yoga classes for mood elevation.

Outcome: Reduction in stress levels due to endorphin release.

Healthy Lifestyle Choices: Emphasizing balanced diet, sufficient sleep, and limiting caffeine intake.

Outcome: Better physical health and stress management.

Seeking Support: Discussing stress with colleagues, supervisor, and seeking professional counseling.

Outcome: Enhanced support network and coping strategies.

Creating a Positive Work Environment: Setting clear job expectations, offering development opportunities, and encouraging communication.

Outcome: Reduced role ambiguity and a supportive work setting.

Setting Boundaries: Establishing work-life boundaries for improved relaxation.

Outcome: Enhanced personal time rejuvenation.

Mindfulness and Meditation: Practicing mindfulness throughout the workday for focus and tranquility.

Outcome: Reduced stress and enhanced well-being.

Stress Management Training: Providing stress management training covering coping strategies.

Outcome: Equipping employees with tools for stress management.

Flexible Work Arrangements: Offering flexible work options like remote work to aid work-life balance.

Outcome: Reduced stress levels and enhanced job satisfaction.

By identifying Swati's stress sources and implementing diverse stress management strategies, both Swati and TechSolutions Inc. achieved significant stress reduction, improved well-being, and enhanced productivity. This case study highlights the value of proactive stress management and its positive impact on mental and physical health, as well as organizational success.

CONCLUSION

Workplace stress is a prevalent aspect of modern life, but it can be managed effectively. By recognizing sources of stress and their impact, employees and employers can proactively address stress. Utilizing stress management techniques such as time management, relaxation, physical activity, and seeking support can significantly enhance well-being and productivity. Establishing a positive work environment and supporting stress management efforts can lead to a healthier, more content, and productive workforce.

-------------- Multiple Choice Type Questions --------------

Q1. What is highlighted as one of the primary sources of stress in the workplace?

A. Job Security
B. Role Ambiguity
C. Environmental Factors
D. Workload

Q2. What impact can stress have on an employee's performance?

A. Increased productivity
B. Enhanced decision-making
C. Lower output and increased errors
D. Improved work quality

Q3. Which stress management strategy involves practices like deep breathing and meditation?

A. Time Management
B. Seeking Support
C. Mindfulness and Meditation
D. Physical Activity

Q4. What is emphasized as critical for stress management in the text?

A. Overworking
B. Lack of breaks
C. Healthy lifestyle choices
D. All of the above

Q5. How can employers aid in stress reduction?

A. By increasing workload
B. By recognizing achievements
C. By setting unclear job expectations
D. By resolving conflicts

Q6. Which stress management technique involves setting clear job expectations and offering professional development?

A. Time Management
B. Stress Management Training
C. Setting Boundaries
D. Creating a Positive Work Environment

Q7. What can stress management training equip employees with?

A. Increased workload
B. Tools for effective stress handling
C. Limited access to resources
D. Reduced communication with colleagues

Q8. What is recommended for establishing a healthier work-life balance?

A. Constantly checking work emails during personal time
B. Avoiding breaks and relaxation activities
C. Disengaging from work during non-working hours
E. Increasing work hours without breaks

------------------- Match The Following -------------------

Q1. Match the following stress management strategies with their descriptions:

1. Time Management	A. Maintaining a balanced diet, adequate sleep, and healthy habits.
2. Relaxation Techniques	B. Maintaining a supportive and encouraging work atmosphere.
3. Physical Activity	C. Openly discussing stress with colleagues, supervisors, or professionals.
4. Healthy Lifestyle Choices	D. Establishing limits between work and personal life.
5. Seeking Support	E. Techniques to maintain focus and reduce stress.
6. Creating a Positive Work Environment	F. Equipping employees with tools for effective stress handling.
7. Setting Boundaries	G. Practices to promote relaxation and mental well-being.
8. Mindfulness and Meditation	H. Offering options for work-life balance.
9. Stress Management Training	I. Efficient time organization and task prioritization.
10. Flexible Work Arrangements	J. Engaging in regular exercise for stress relief.

Q2. Match the following impacts of stress with their consequences:

1. Decreased Productivity	A. More sick days taken due to health issues related to stress.
2. Poor Quality of Work	B. Difficulty in cooperation and teamwork.
3. Increased Absenteeism	C. Employee disengagement and lack of motivation.
4. Lower Morale	D. Reduced output and increased errors.
5. Strained Relationships	E. Compromised task accuracy and detail management.

CHAPTER 4

DEPRESSION MANAGEMENT

INTRODUCTION

Depression, a prevalent yet severe mood disorder, influences an individual's emotions, thoughts, and daily functioning. It can lead to emotional and physical challenges, hindering one's work and personal life. Effective management is crucial in enhancing the well-being of those struggle with depression. This section delves into diverse strategies for handling depression, underpinned by real-life illustrations.

Ensure to respond to each question provided at the conclusion of the chapter. This will allow you to assess your knowledge of the subject matter and determine if you require a brief refresher or a more thorough reading.

UNDERSTANDING DEPRESSION

Depression, also referred to as major depressive disorder, manifests as enduring sadness, loss of interest in once-enjoyed activities, and a spectrum of emotional and physical symptoms. These changes in appetite, sleep disruptions, fatigue, feelings of worthlessness, difficulty concentrating, and thoughts of self-harm. Grasping the intricate nature of depression is paramount in its effective management.

DEPRESSION MANAGEMENT APPROACHES

Medical Intervention

Typically, medical treatment for depression revolves around antidepressants that help regulate mood-affecting brain chemicals.

Example: Surekha, a 35-year-old graphic designer, battled severe depression post a traumatic incident. Her psychiatrist prescribed an SSRI (Selective Serotonin Reuptake Inhibitor), leading to mood stabilization. With regular monitoring, Surekha's depressive symptoms significantly alleviated, enabling her to resume work and relish life once more.

Psychotherapy

Psychotherapy, notably Cognitive Behavioural Therapy (CBT) and Interpersonal Therapy (IPT), stands as a cornerstone in depression management, assisting individuals in transforming thought patterns and behaviours.

Example: John, a 42-year-old engineer, struggled with depression after a job loss. Through CBT, John learned to identify and combat negative thoughts, promoting healthier coping mechanisms. This therapy proved pivotal in rebuilding his confidence and drive to pursue new job opportunities.

Lifestyle Adjustments

In managing depression, lifestyle changes like regular physical activity, a balanced diet, ample sleep, and stress reduction techniques can enhance symptoms.

Example: Emily, a 28-year-old teacher, discovered that incorporating daily exercise, mindfulness meditation, and a balanced diet eased her depressive symptoms. Establishing a consistent sleep regimen notably uplifted her mood and energy levels.

Social Support

Robust social support networks are critical in depression management, offering emotional backing and reducing feelings of isolation.

Example: Post experiencing postpartum depression, Maria, a new mother, engaged with a local support group for new parents. Sharing and listening to others' experiences lessened her sense of solitude, providing practical guidance and emotional solace, essential in her recovery.

Alternative Therapies

Complementary therapies like acupuncture, yoga, and herbal supplements may augment conventional treatments in managing depression for some individuals.

Example: David, a 50-year-old businessman, found a reprieve from depressive symptoms through regular yoga sessions and acupuncture. These therapies complemented his conventional treatment, offering additional benefits in relaxation and stress reduction.

CASE STUDY 1: HOLISTIC DEPRESSION MANAGEMENT

Rebecca, a 30-year-old lawyer, suffered with severe depression post a personal loss. Her comprehensive treatment plan entailed:

Medication: Prescribed an antidepressant by her psychiatrist.

Therapy: Attended weekly CBT sessions targeting negative thought patterns.

Lifestyle Changes: Incorporated daily exercise, healthy eating, and ensured sufficient sleep.

Social Support: Leaned on friends and family for emotional backing, also participating in a grief support group.

Alternative Therapies: Practiced mindfulness meditation and attended occasional acupuncture sessions.

By combining varying approaches, Rebecca witnessed gradual improvement. She acquired effective symptom management skills, reclaiming her capacity to function in personal and professional spheres.

CASE STUDY 2: FROM DEPRESSED TO DYNAMIC: BLESSED TO BE STRESSED

Depression and stress are closely linked. Stress can lead to symptoms of depression. Prolonged exposure to stressful situations exhausts the body's coping mechanisms, often resulting in feelings of hopelessness and sadness. Managing stress effectively is therefore crucial to prevent it from escalating into depression. This case study shows how an employee with too much work stayed positive. Instead of getting stressed and depressed, he turned the challenge into a chance to prove himself and succeed in his career.

In various cultures and faith traditions, when individuals present flowers to deities, they opt for the most exquisite and flawless blooms. This gesture symbolizes offering the finest they possess to the divine, demonstrating reverence and seeking favour. Likewise, in professional settings, when a boss or leader delegates critical tasks to an individual, it signifies that they view that person as the "cream of the crop" within their team – someone who is highly capable, reliable, and worthy of handling important matters. The expression "You are blessed to be stressed" describes the notion that being entrusted with significant responsibilities and tasks, despite being stressful, is actually an indication of trust and acknowledgment of one's abilities and potential. This philosophy suggests that if you are consistently tasked with pivotal assignments, it is because you are perceived as the most competent and dependable individual available, much like how the finest flower is chosen for offerings in a religious context.

In a corporate environment, Avirup, a project manager, is frequently entrusted with challenging projects and tasked with leading key client meetings by his boss leading to possible depression. Despite the resulting long hours and significant stress, Avirup's consistent selection for these critical tasks is not arbitrary.

Key Client Presentation

Situation: A crucial client presentation is impending, carrying the potential for a multi-million-dollar deal.

Boss's Decision: Avirup is designated to spearhead the presentation.

Reason: Avirup's history of delivering captivating presentations and securing deals makes him the optimal choice.

New Product Launch

Situation: The company is on the brink of launching a ground-breaking new product.

Boss's Decision: Avirup is entrusted with overseeing the entire launch event.

Reason: Avirup's exceptional organizational acumen and successful management of similar events in the past justify his selection.

Crisis Management

Situation: An unforeseen issue jeopardizes the timeline of a major project.

Boss's Decision: Avirup is tasked with resolving the crisis.

Reason: Avirup's adept problem-solving skills and track record of salvaging troubled projects support his appointment.

Analysis

Despite Avirup's feelings of stress due to the demanding nature of his role, his boss's consistent reliance on him for pivotal responsibilities underscores his competencies and the faith reposed in him. Like a fine flower chosen for an esteemed offering, Avirup is repeatedly selected as he shines as the prime candidate.

The adage "You are blessed to be stressed" champions a constructive outlook on stress and accountability, emphasizing that being handpicked for arduous tasks signifies distinction, showcasing one's strengths and the confidence others have in them. Just as the finest bloom is earmarked for the divine, individuals with exceptional capabilities are tapped for weighty duties, spotlighting their value and potential for development.

CONCLUSION

Effective depression management necessitates a tailored, multifaceted strategy matching individual needs. Medical intervention, psychotherapy, lifestyle adjustments, social support, and alternative therapies collectively aid individuals in navigating and conquering depression. By understanding and leveraging these strategies, those impacted by depression can strive towards recovery and enhance their overall quality of life.

-------------- **Multiple Choice Type Questions** --------------

Q1. Depression, also referred to as major depressive disorder, manifests as:

A. Temporary sadness

B. Enduring happiness

C. Enduring sadness, loss of interest in once-enjoyed activities, and a spectrum of emotional and physical symptoms

D. Temporary joy and excitement

Q2. What typically revolves around antidepressants that help regulate mood-affecting brain chemicals?

A. Social Support

B. Medical Intervention

C. Lifestyle Adjustments

D. Alternative Therapies

Q3. Which type of therapy is a cornerstone in depression management, assisting individuals in transforming thought patterns and behaviours?

A. Lifestyle Adjustments

B. Medical Intervention

C. Psychotherapy

D. Social Support

Q4. Which of the following is NOT a part of lifestyle adjustments for managing depression?

A. Regular physical activity

B. Balanced diet

C. Ample sleep

D. Antidepressants

Q5. Why are robust social support networks critical in managing depression?

A. They offer emotional backing and reduce feelings of isolation.

B. They regulate brain chemicals.

C. They replace the need for medical intervention.

D. They are part of psychotherapy techniques.

Q6. Which of the following is an example of alternative therapies that may supplement conventional treatments in managing depression?

A. CBT and IPT

B. Yoga and acupuncture

C. Social support groups

D. Regular physical activity

-------------------- **Match The Following** --------------------

Q1. Match the following depression management approaches with their descriptions:

1. Lifestyle Adjustments	A. Regulating mood-affecting brain chemicals with antidepressants.
2. Alternative Therapies	B. Assisting individuals in transforming thought patterns and behaviours through methods like CBT and IPT.
3. Social Support	C. Incorporating daily exercise, a balanced diet, ample sleep, and stress reduction techniques to enhance symptoms.
4. Psychotherapy	D. Engaging with robust social support networks to offer emotional backing and reduce feelings of isolation.
5. Medical Intervention	E. Using acupuncture, yoga, and herbal supplements as complementary treatments.

CHAPTER 5

PRESENTATIONS SKILLS

INTRODUCTION

An impactful presentation leverages the connection between the speaker and the audience. It thoroughly considers the audience's needs to captivate their interest, enhance their comprehension, boost their confidence, and achieve the speaker's objectives. Mastering public speaking is a challenging task. The key to delivering a presentation lies in meticulous preparation, steady delivery on the actual day, and enthusiasm for the subject matter. Remember, presenting isn't solely about addressing a large crowd it also applies to one-on-one presentations to superiors, which are essential for your career growth and demand similar competencies. Clearly and effectively conveying information is a vital skill for articulating your viewpoint, and nowadays, presentation skills are indispensable across various fields. Whether you are a student, administrator, or executive aiming to launch your own venture, secure funding, or run for an elected position, you might find yourself called upon to deliver a presentation.

Please answer to each question provided at the conclusion of the chapter. This will allow you to assess your knowledge of the subject matter and determine if you require a brief refresher or a more thorough reading.

UNDERSTANDING PRESENTATION SKILLS

Presentation skills contain communication abilities that can be adapted to diverse speaking scenarios like addressing a group, participating in a meeting, or briefing a team. A presentation is a broad term that also includes other 'speaking engagements' such as delivering a toast at a wedding or making a point in a video conference. Effective presentations necessitate thorough preparation, meticulous consideration of the method and tools for delivering information. The goal is to convey a message to the audience and often involves a 'persuasive' component. For instance, the presentation could focus on highlighting your organization's positive impact, showcasing your value to an employer, or justifying the need for additional funding for a project.

STRUCTURING YOUR PRESENTATION

Establishing Goals

Define the purpose of your presentation and select a compelling subject or topic. Illustrate how your topic is relevant to the audience. Well-defined objectives will help you stay on track and ensure your presentation has a clear trajectory and purpose.

Understanding Your Audience

Take into account the audience's demographics, including age, gender, culture, and professional background. Employ examples that resonate with the audience and use appropriate language, avoiding excessive jargon. Ensure you can articulate each word in your speech correctly. Tailoring your message to your audience's interests and comprehension level enhances the impact and engagement of your presentation.

Developing Content & Presentation Structure

Begin by outlining the key points you aim to cover. Seamless transitions between related points facilitate a smooth flow of your presentation. Flesh out sub-points and supporting materials to reinforce your main points. Organize your content logically to help the audience follow your line of reasoning and retain the information shared.

OVERCOMING STAGE ANXIETY

It's common to experience apprehension when speaking in front of an audience. However, much like other fears, stage fright can be conquered with guidance and practice. Here are some strategies to help you navigate this fear.

Acknowledge Your Nervousness

Embrace the fact that you may feel nervous when speaking formally.

Recognize Physical Reactions

Acknowledge that nervousness triggers a surge of adrenaline, resulting in physical sensations.

Embrace Positive Energy

Understand that heightened adrenaline levels provide you with extra energy.

Harness Nervous Energy

View nervousness as a beneficial force that you can leverage to your advantage.

Normalize Nervousness

Remember that feeling nervous is common among individuals who perform in professional settings, including actors, singers, and politicians.

Employ Positive Visualization

Envision yourself delivering a powerful and confident presentation. Positive imagery instils a sense of freshness and assurance.

Preparation is Key

Invest significant effort in preparing your content. Proper preparation will boost your enthusiasm for sharing your knowledge with others.

Focus on the Introduction

Give special attention to crafting engaging opening lines and a captivating introduction. Incorporate humour and wit when appropriate, as nervousness is most palpable at the start of a presentation.

Engage with Your Audience

Establish eye contact with your audience members to feel connected and rooted in the presentation.

Practice is Essential

Rehearse your presentation in front of friends, family, or peers. Regular practice hones your performance and bolsters your confidence.

Display Warmth and Smile

Begin your presentation with a warm smile, akin to engaging in activities you genuinely enjoy.

CASE STUDY: ENHANCING PRESENTATION SKILLS FOR CAREER PROGRESSION

Overview

Anvesha, a project manager at a mid-sized tech firm, showcases exceptional project management skills but fears with public speaking. Given her increasing need to present to senior management and potential clients, Anvesha recognizes the pivotal role of presentation skills in her career growth and endeavors to enhance this crucial ability.

Scenario

Assigned with presenting a new software product to potential investors, Anvesha faces a critical juncture in securing funding for her company. Motivated to deliver a presentation highlighting the product's value, Anvesha is determined to excel in this high-pressure situation.

Understanding Effective Presentations

Commencing her journey by researching effective presentation strategies, Anvesha learns that presentation skills contain varied communication abilities adaptable to diverse speaking scenarios like group addresses, meetings, and briefings. The core aim of a presentation is to convey a message persuasively.

Structuring the Presentation

Defining Objectives: Anvesha outlines her presentation's purpose: securing funding for the new software product. Selecting a subject that accentuates the product's innovative features and market potential. Establishing clear objectives to maintain focus and provide the presentation with a definitive direction.

Audience Analysis: Tailoring her message to resonate with potential investors' backgrounds and interests. Practicing clear articulation for effective communication devoid of technical jargon.

Content Development and Presentation Flow: Outlining key talking points with seamless transitions.

Crafting sub-points and supportive materials to reinforce the main message, organizing content logically for audience comprehension.

Overcoming Presentation Anxiety

Embracing Nervousness: Acknowledging and accepting the natural nerves associated with public speaking.

Channeling Nervous Energy: Reframing nerves as a source of beneficial energy, leveraging positive visualization techniques for confident delivery.

Preparation and Rehearsal: Diligent preparation to boost enthusiasm in sharing knowledge. Crafting engaging openings, incorporating humor for a relaxed start. Rehearsing in front of peers to refine performance and build confidence.

Audience Engagement

Establishing eye contact, exhibiting warmth and confidence with a welcoming smile at the beginning of the presentation.

Outcome: Anvesha's meticulous preparation and polished delivery culminate in a compelling presentation effectively showcasing the new software product's value. Impressed by her confidence and clarity, potential investors readily provide the necessary funding, underscoring the success of Anvesha's presentation.

Anvesha's journey underscores the significance of honing presentation skills for career advancement. Through tailored content, thorough preparation, and strategies to combat stage anxiety, she not only advances her professional trajectory but also contributes to her company's success. This case study epitomizes the transformative impact of mastering presentation skills on career growth and achieving professional milestones.

CONCLUSION

Communication skills are consistently highlighted as a critical aspect by nearly all organizations, with presentation skills being a significant component of effective communication. These skills play a vital role in academic and business realms, spanning from meetings and job interviews to conferences. Oftentimes, leadership and presentation skills are intertwined. Effective presentation skills empower you to articulate ideas clearly, engage your audience effectively, and accomplish your objectives. Strengthening your presentation skills enhances your ability to persuade, inform, and inspire others. Whether addressing a small group or a large audience, mastering these skills can significantly impact your professional and personal achievements. By understanding presentation skills, you equip yourself to communicate more effectively and become a better presenter, unlocking new prospects and achieving greater success in your pursuits.

-------------- Multiple Choice Type Questions --------------

Q1. Which of the following is essential for delivering a compelling presentation?

A. Impromptu speaking
B. Thorough preparation
C. Casual conversation
D. Improvisation

Q2. What is a key element in understanding your audience?

A. Using excessive jargon
B. Considering the audience's demographics
C. Focusing solely on the speaker's interests
D. Ignoring the audience's background

Q3. What should you focus on to boost your enthusiasm and confidence in your presentation?

A. Spontaneity
B. Extensive preparation
C. Avoiding practice
D. Ignoring the introduction

Q4. Which strategy involves envisioning yourself delivering a powerful and confident presentation?

    A. Acknowledge Your Nervousness
    B. Embrace Positive Energy
    C. Employ Positive Visualization
    D. Recognize Physical Reactions

Q5. What is one of the benefits of establishing eye contact with your audience?

    A. Feeling disconnected
    B. Enhancing nervousness
    C. Feeling connected and rooted in the presentation
    D. Distracting the audience

Q6. What does structuring your presentation involve?

    A. Ignoring the audience's interests
    B. Outlining key points and ensuring smooth transitions
    C. Focusing on unrelated topics
    D. Using complex language and jargon

Q7. Which component is NOT part of the essential presentation skills mentioned?

    A. Communication abilities
    B. Persuasive components
    C. Avoiding thorough preparation
    D. Adapting to diverse speaking scenarios

Q8. What should be the focus of your presentation introduction?

    A. Using technical terms
    B. Crafting engaging opening lines and incorporating humour when appropriate
    C. Avoiding eye contact
    D. Ignoring the audience

-------------------- Match The Following --------------------

Q1. Match the following strategies for overcoming stage anxiety with their descriptions:

1. Acknowledge Your Nervousness	A. Understand that heightened adrenaline levels provide extra energy.
2. Recognize Physical Reactions	B. Acknowledge that nervousness triggers a surge of adrenaline, resulting in physical sensations.
3. Embrace Positive Energy	C. Invest significant effort in preparing your content to boost enthusiasm.
4. Harness Nervous Energy	D. Embrace the fact that you may feel nervous when speaking formally.
5. Normalize Nervousness	E. View nervousness as a beneficial force that can be leveraged to your advantage.
6. Employ Positive Visualization	F. Give special attention to crafting engaging opening lines and a captivating introduction.
7. Preparation is Key	G. Remember that feeling nervous is common among performers like actors and politicians.
8. Focus on the Introduction	H. Envision yourself delivering a powerful and confident presentation.

Q2. Match the following components of structuring a presentation with their descriptions:

1. Establishing Goals	A. Outline key points, ensure smooth transitions, and organize content logically.
2. Understanding Your Audience	B. Consider the audience's demographics and tailor your message to their interests and comprehension level.
3. Developing Content & Presentation Structure	C. Define the purpose of your presentation and select a compelling subject.

CHAPTER 6

SITUATIONAL AWARENESS

INTRODUCTION

Situational Awareness (SA) refers to the capacity to perceive and comprehend elements in the surrounding environment within a specific time and space, estimating their status in the near future. At its core, SA enables quick and effective action by enhancing your orientation and understanding of the environment. This chapter explores the fundamental principles and tools that boost situational awareness, such as the Cooper Color Codes, the Observe Orient Decide Act (OODA) Loop, and Situational Leadership, offering a comprehensive tool for sustaining awareness and making well-informed decisions.

Make sure to answer all the questions given at the end of the chapter. This will help you evaluate your understanding of the subject and decide if you need a quick refresh or a more comprehensive review.

COOPER COLOR CODES

The Cooper Color Codes, devised by Colonel Jeff Cooper, comprise a set of principles concerning SA that gained popularity among individuals interested in self-defense. These codes aid in understanding how individuals process danger and develop strategies to heighten awareness. The four color codes: White, Yellow, Orange, and Red depict varying levels of awareness and readiness.

White

Condition White signifies a state of complete unawareness and unreadiness. Individuals in this state are oblivious to their surroundings and highly susceptible to attacks. This level of awareness is the most perilous, leaving a person entirely unprepared to react to any threats.

Yellow

Condition Yellow represents a state of "Relaxed Alert," where there is no immediate, evident threat, but the individual acknowledges the constant possibility of danger. Individuals in this state are conscious of their environment and the people around them. This level of awareness is ideal for everyday life, enabling preparedness without paranoia.

Orange

Condition Orange denotes an elevated state of awareness where an individual identifies or becomes aware of a specific threat. In this condition, individuals start formulating potential responses to address the danger. For instance, if one notices someone suspiciously trailing them, they would be in Condition Orange, readying themselves for potential action.

Red

Condition Red involves taking action. This heightened awareness level results from transitioning from Condition Orange to actively engaging with or evading the threat. It embodies the "Fight or Flight" response and demands complete mental and physical dedication to the immediate peril. This phase is both physically and mentally draining.

Black

Researchers later introduced Condition Black, symbolizing a state of mental paralysis or freezing under pressure. In this status, an individual is immobilized by fear or confusion, rendering them incapable of responding to the threat. The objective is to avoid reaching Condition Black by maintaining a state of Condition Yellow, where one remains aware of their surroundings and prepared to act if necessary.

Sustaining Condition Yellow in daily life necessitates initial conscientious effort, which with practice, becomes second nature. Regardless of navigating rush-hour traffic or encountering personal protection situations, staying in Condition Yellow enables you to comprehend your surroundings and know how to respond when things deviate.

OODA LOOP

The OODA Loop, crafted by military strategist John Boyd, elucidates how individuals and organizations can succeed in ambiguous scenarios. Standing for Observe, Orient, Decide, and Act, the OODA Loop serves as a framework for adapting to and learning from various situations, rather than just a decision-making tool.

Observe

The initial phase, Observe, involves actively absorbing the entire scenario. This contains comprehending one's own situation, the competitors' positions, and the environment. It acts as the primary data collection phase, where one evaluates their position in the environment, the competitors' stances, environmental shifts, and potential future scenarios.

Orient

Orient constitutes the most crucial step in the loop. It entails analyzing and synthesizing the observations made. This phase demands judgment, intuition, and experience to comprehend the myriad factors around you, rendering the outcome unpredictable. Orientation aids in grasping the context and implications of the observations.

Decide

The Decide step bridges the gap between orientation and action, essentially involving the selection of the optimal course of action based on the analysis conducted. This decision-making phase sets the stage for subsequent actions.

Act

The Act stage involves executing the decision made. Upon acting, the OODA Loop recommences, ensuring a continuous process of enhancement, learning, and adaptation. The crux of success lies in remaining in the loop and consistently refining one's comprehension and responses.

The OODA Loop's applications are universal, extending from personal lives to solving business challenges. By perpetually operating within the loop and translating decisions into actions, individuals and organizations can elevate their situational awareness and adaptability.

SITUATIONAL LEADERSHIP AND ITS APPLICATIONS

Situational Leadership theory, developed by Dr. Paul Hersey and Ken Blanchard, focuses on tailoring leadership approaches based on the maturity and skills of team members. The theory advocates that effective leaders should adjust their leadership styles according to follower maturity and task specifics.

Leadership Styles

According to Hersey and Blanchard's Situational Leadership Theory, there exist four primary leadership styles:

S1: Telling/Directing

Leaders instruct team members on what to do and how to do it, suitable for followers who lack skills or confidence.

S2: Selling/Coaching

Leaders offer guidance, communicate with followers, and rally support, benefiting followers willing but lacking skills.

S3: Participating/Consulting

Leaders emphasize teamwork and shared decision-making, ideal for skilled but hesitant followers.

S4: Delegating

Leaders assign responsibility to followers, overseeing progress while allowing autonomy, ideal for highly skilled and confident followers.

Maturity Levels

Hersey and Blanchard categorize followers into four maturity levels:

M1

Those at this level require guidance due to insufficient skills or confidence.

M2

Followers willing to work but lacking necessary skills.

M3

Followers with skills but lacking self-assurance.

M4

Highly skilled and confident followers capable of independent work.

The model aligns each leadership style with a corresponding maturity level, facilitating effective team guidance.

EXAMPLES

Example 1: Suppose you assign tasks to a capable colleague before a holiday and micromanage the process. Your colleague, an M4 in maturity, warranted a more hands-off leadership approach.

Example 2: Leading a new team with mixed skills and enthusiasm, applying an S3 leadership style to coach and empower. By estimating their maturity level at M3, a collaborative approach inculcates team relationships and success.

CASE STUDY: METRO CITY POLICE DEPARTMENT

Problem Statement

The Metro City Police Department (MCPD) faced challenges with officers' situational awareness during patrols. Several incidents of ambush attacks and missed opportunities to prevent crimes indicated a need for improved readiness and response strategies.

Implementation Plan

Training Program Development: MCPD collaborated with a tactical training expert to develop a comprehensive training program based on Cooper Color Codes.The program included classroom sessions, practical exercises, and scenariobased drills to familiarize officers with the different conditions and appropriate responses.

Integration with Daily Operations: Officers were trained to use Cooper Color Codes during their daily patrols. Dispatchers and supervisors were also trained to use the codes to communicate effectively with patrol officers. A standard operating procedure (SOP) was established, outlining the use of color codes during routine and highrisk situations.

Assessment and Feedback: Regular assessments were conducted to evaluate officers' understanding and application of Cooper Color Codes. Feedback sessions were held to discuss experiences, challenges, and improvements.

Color Codes Overview

Condition White: Unaware and unprepared.

Example: An officer distracted by personal thoughts while on patrol.

Condition Yellow: Relaxed alertness.

Example: An officer observing surroundings and maintaining awareness during a routine patrol.

Condition Orange: Specific alert.

Example: An officer identifies a potential threat, such as suspicious behavior, and focuses attention on it while preparing to act.

Condition Red: Specific threat identified and action is imminent.

Example: An officer draws a weapon and prepares to confront an armed suspect.

Condition Black: Imminent danger requiring immediate action.

Example: An officer engages in a firefight or an active shooter situation.

Outcomes

Enhanced Situational Awareness: Officers reported an increased ability to detect potential threats early and respond appropriately. There was a notable decrease in ambush attacks on officers.

Improved Response Times: The clear communication of threat levels using color codes improved coordination between officers and dispatchers. Response times to highrisk incidents were significantly reduced.

Reduction in Incidents: The proactive use of Condition Yellow and Condition Orange allowed officers to prevent crimes before they escalated. The department recorded a 20% decrease in violent crimes during patrols.

Officer Safety and Confidence: Officers felt more confident in their ability to handle various situations. The structured approach to threat assessment and response contributed to a safer working environment.

The implementation of Cooper Color Codes in the Metro City Police Department successfully enhanced situational awareness, improved response times, and reduced incidents of violent crimes. This case study demonstrates the practical application of Cooper Color Codes in law enforcement and highlights the importance of training, integration, and continuous assessment in achieving these outcomes.

Recommendations

Continuous Training: Regular refresher courses and scenario based drills should be conducted to maintain officers' proficiency in using Cooper Color Codes.

Integration with Technology: Incorporate the use of body cameras and mobile devices to support realtime communication and documentation of situational awareness levels.

Expand Implementation: Consider implementing Cooper Color Codes in other units within the department, to enhance overall readiness and response capabilities.

Community Engagement: Educate the community on the importance of situational awareness and how they can contribute to public safety by reporting suspicious activities.

CONCLUSION

Situational awareness plays a crucial role in personal safety beyond tactical scenarios. By embracing and applying situational awareness principles, individuals can elevate their safety and efficiency across various life domains.

-------------- Multiple Choice Type Questions --------------

Q1. What does Situational Awareness (SA) enable?

A. Enhanced financial decision-making
B. Quick and effective action by understanding the environment
C. Improved social interactions
D. Better long-term planning

Q2. Who devised the Cooper Color Codes?

A. John Boyd
B. Robert Kaplan
C. Dr. Paul Hersey
D. Colonel Jeff Cooper

Q3. Which condition in the Cooper Color Codes signifies a state of complete unawareness and unreadiness?

A. Condition Yellow
B. Condition Orange
C. Condition White
D. Condition Red

Q4. In the Cooper Color Codes, what does Condition Yellow represent?

A. State of complete unawareness
B. State of "Relaxed Alert"
C. Elevated state of awareness
D. Taking action

Q5. What does the OODA Loop stand for?

    A. Observe, Orient, Decide, Act

    B. Overcome, Observe, Decide, Act

    C. Orient, Overcome, Decide, Act

    D. Observe, Overcome, Decide, Act

Q6. Who developed the OODA Loop?

    A. Dr. Paul Hersey

    B. Robert Kaplan

    C. Colonel Jeff Cooper

    D. John Boyd

Q7. In the OODA Loop, what is the initial phase?

    A. Decide

    B. Act

    C. Orient

    D. Observe

Q8. According to Hersey and Blanchard's Situational Leadership Theory, which leadership style is suitable for highly skilled and confident followers?

    A. S1: Telling/Directing

    B. S2: Selling/Coaching

    C. S3: Participating/Consulting

    D. S4: Delegating

Q9. In Situational Leadership, what maturity level corresponds to followers who are willing to work but lack necessary skills?

    A. M1

    B. M2

    C. M3

    D. M4

Q10. What does Condition Black in the Cooper Color Codes symbolize?

A. Elevated state of awareness

B. Mental paralysis or freezing under pressure

C. Complete unawareness

D. State of "Relaxed Alert"

-------------------- Match The Following --------------------

Q1. Match the following Situational Leadership styles with their descriptions:

1. S1: Telling/Directing	A. Leaders emphasize teamwork and shared decision-making
2. S2: Selling/Coaching	B. Leaders instruct team members on what to do and how to do it.
3. S3: Participating/Consulting	C. Leaders assign responsibility to followers, overseeing progress while allowing autonomy.
4. S4: Delegating	D. Leaders offer guidance and rally support.

Q2. Match the following Cooper Color Codes with their descriptions:

1. Condition White	A. State of "Relaxed Alert.
2. Condition Yellow	B. State of complete unawareness and unreadiness
3. Condition Orange	C. Elevated state of awareness with a specific threat identified
4. Condition Red	D. Taking action, "Fight or Flight" response
5. Condition Black	E. State of mental paralysis or freezing under pressure

CHAPTER 7

COMMUNICATION PROFICIENCY

INTRODUCTION

Effective communication serves as the foundation of successful relationships, whether personal or professional. It contains not just the words expressed, but also their delivery and interpretation. This chapter delves into various aspects of communication, including different channels and obstacles, the impact of non-verbal cues, successful communication strategies, and the influence of technology on communication.

Please respond to all the questions provided at the conclusion of the chapter. This will allow you to assess your comprehension of the topic and determine whether a brief recap or a more thorough reading is necessary.

EXPLORING COMMUNICATION CHANNELS AND HURDLES

Communication Channels

Communication channels are the platforms through which information is conveyed. These can be broadly categorized as follows.

Verbal Communication: Involving spoken words, whether in person, via phone calls, or video chats. It enables direct interaction and immediate feedback.

Written Communication: Containing emails, letters, reports, and text messages. It aids in maintaining a record of information and provides time for the recipient to process before responding.

Visual Communication: Utilizing visual aids such as graphs, charts, logos, and videos to efficiently convey information.

Non-verbal Communication: Involving body language, facial expressions, gestures, and eye contact. It complements verbal communication and conveys emotions and attitudes.

Communication Hurdles

Despite the array of channels available, effective communication may face several impediments.

Physical Barriers: Including distance and physical obstacles that can disrupt message transmission. For instance, poor internet connectivity can hinder video calls.

Language Barriers: Variances in language or vocabulary can lead to misunderstandings. Technical jargon or complex terms may also confuse the recipient.

Psychological Barriers: Involving personal elements like stress, anger, or mistrust that impact message delivery and reception.

Cultural Barriers: Differences in cultural backgrounds may result in misinterpretations. Customs considered acceptable in one culture might not be so in another.

Perceptual Barriers: Arising from differences in perception and viewpoints. Individuals may interpret the same message differently based on their experiences and biases.

THE ROLE OF NON-VERBAL COMMUNICATION

Non-verbal communication acts as a potent enhancer of verbal interactions. It comprises of the following:

Body Language

Surrounding posture, movements, and gestures. For instance, crossed arms might signal defensiveness, while an open posture suggests receptivity.

Facial Expressions

Expressing a spectrum of emotions like happiness, anger, sadness, or surprise. A smile often communicates warmth and approval.

Eye Contact

Maintaining eye contact conveys confidence and attentiveness, while its absence might indicate discomfort or disinterest.

Gestures

Hand movements emphasize points and share enthusiasm. It's essential to note that gestures can hold varying meanings in different cultures.

Tone of Voice

The manner in which something is said holds significance alongside the actual words. Tone, pitch, and volume communicate emotions and attitudes.

STRATEGIES FOR EFFECTIVE COMMUNICATION

To enhance communication efficiency, consider the following strategies.

Active Listening

Fully engage with the speaker, acknowledge their message, and respond thoughtfully. Avoid interruptions and demonstrate your engagement through gestures or verbal cues like "I see" or "I understand."

Clarity and Conciseness

Be explicit and succinct. Avoid using technical terms or intricate language. Simplicity and directness provide better understanding and minimize misinterpretation.

Empathy

Strive to understand the emotions and perspectives of others. Empathetic communication generate trust and rapport.

Feedback

Offer constructive feedback and be open to receiving it. Feedback aids in clarifying misconceptions and refining communication.

Appropriate Medium

Select the suitable communication channel for your message. For instance, sensitive information may be best conveyed in person, while routine updates can be communicated via email.

Non-verbal Cues

Be mindful of your body language, facial expressions, and tone of voice. Ensure that your non-verbal signals align with your verbal messages.

IMPACT OF TECHNOLOGY ON COMMUNICATION

Technology has transformed communication methods, presenting both benefits and obstacles.

Advantages

Speed and Efficiency: Technology enables instant communication through emails, instant messaging, and video calls, facilitating swift information sharing.

Accessibility: Individuals can communicate globally, surmounting geographical barriers. This is especially advantageous for remote teams and international enterprises.

Multimedia: Technology permits the use of multimedia features such as videos, images, and interactive elements, enhancing communication effectiveness.

Record Keeping: Digital communication allows for effortless record-keeping and information retrieval, beneficial for reference and documentation.

Challenges

Overload: The overflow of emails, messages, and notifications can result in information overload, obstructing focus on critical tasks.

Misinterpretation: Written communication devoid of non-verbal cues may be misinterpreted at times. Tone and context can be lost in text-based messages.

Dependence on Technology: Excessive reliance on technology may reduce face-to-face interactions, vital for ensuring robust relationships and trust.

Security and Privacy: Digital communication is susceptible to security breaches and privacy issues. Using secure channels and being cautious while sharing sensitive data is paramount.

CASE STUDY: IMPROVING COMMUNICATION EFFECTIVENESS WITHIN A DIVERSE TEAM

Background

Surekha, a project manager at a global marketing firm, leads a diverse team spread across different time zones and cultures. Efficient communication is crucial for her role. Recently, her team encountered difficulties in coordinating projects, leading to missed deadlines and misunderstandings. Recognizing the urgency for improved communication skills, Surekha took steps to analyze and tackle these challenges.

Scenario

Surekha's team is currently engaged in a marketing campaign for a key client, comprising members from the US, India, and Germany. Despite regular meetings and updates, they faced recurring issues such as misinterpretations and task delays. Surekha pinpointed language barriers, cultural disparities, and an excessive reliance on written communication as the primary communication obstacles.

Investigating Communication Channels and Obstacles

Identifying the tools used by her team for communication like emails, video calls, and a project management platform, Surekha noted the following obstacles.

Language Barriers: Some team members struggled with understanding complex jargon and technical terms in emails.

Cultural Barriers: Variances in communication styles sparked misinterpretations. For example, direct feedback from German team members was perceived as overly blunt by their American counterparts.

Over-reliance on Written Communication: Vital nuances were lost in email exchanges, causing confusion.

The Significance of Non-Verbal Communication

Recognizing the role of non-verbal cues in bridging gaps, Surekha encouraged more video calls to leverage body language, facial expressions, and tone of voice. This approach enabled team members to better comprehend each other's emotions and attitudes.

Effective Communication Strategies

To enhance communication within the team, Surekha implemented the following strategies.

Active Listening: She emphasized active listening during meetings to ensure team members felt acknowledged and understood.

Clarity and Conciseness: Surekha promoted clear and simple communication, avoiding overly technical language and jargon.

Empathy: Surekha facilitated discussions on cultural differences and encouraged mutual understanding.

Feedback: Regular feedback sessions were introduced to promptly address and resolve misunderstandings.

Appropriate Medium: Sensitive information was shared through video calls, while routine updates were conveyed via email.

Impact of Technology on Communication

Leveraging technology to enhance communication, Surekha acknowledged both its benefits and challenges.

Advantages: Video calls and collaborative tools improved real-time communication and information sharing.

Challenges: Addressing the risk of information overload, she established clear guidelines for email usage and stressed the importance of face-to-face interactions for crucial discussions.

Outcome

By incorporating these strategies, Surekha's team experienced notable progress in communication effectiveness. Misunderstandings decreased, deadlines were met, and team cohesion strengthened. This case study underscores the significance of comprehending communication channels, non-verbal cues, and strategic technology utilization to enhance communication proficiency within a diverse team.

CONCLUSION

Enhancing communication proficiency is crucial for personal and professional prosperity. Understanding diverse communication channels and barriers aids in selecting the appropriate medium and overcoming hindrances. Non-verbal cues play a pivotal role in reinforcing verbal messages and conveying emotions. Effective communication strategies like active listening, clarity, empathy, feedback, and selecting the right medium can elevate the quality of interactions. Embracing technology judiciously can augment communication efficiency while recognizing and addressing its challenges. By perfecting these skills, one can communicate more effectively and build stronger, more meaningful relationships.

-------------- **Multiple Choice Type Questions** --------------

Q1. Which of the following is NOT a category of communication channels?

A. Verbal Communication
B. Written Communication
C. Visual Communication
D. Emotional Communication

Q2. What type of communication involves spoken words, whether in person, via phone calls, or video chats?

A. Written Communication
B. Non-verbal Communication
C. Verbal Communication
D. Visual Communication

Q3. Which barrier involves variances in language or vocabulary leading to misunderstandings?

A. Physical Barriers
B. Language Barriers
C. Psychological Barriers
D. Cultural Barriers

Q4. What does non-verbal communication NOT typically include?

A. Body language
B. Facial expressions
C. Handwriting
D. Eye contact

Q5. Which strategy for effective communication involves fully engaging with the speaker and acknowledging their message?

A. Empathy
B. Active Listening
C. Feedback
D. Clarity and Conciseness

Q6. Which of the following is an advantage of technology in communication?

A. Misinterpretation of messages
B. Dependence on technology
C. Speed and Efficiency
D. Security and Privacy issues

Q7. Which non-verbal cue involves understanding and sharing others' feelings to build stronger relationships?

A. Eye Contact
B. Gestures
C. Tone of Voice
D. Empathy

Q8. What is a common challenge associated with digital communication?

A. Instant communication
B. Multimedia features
C. Information overload
D. Record keeping

-------------------- **Match The Following** --------------------

Q1. Match the following communication channels with their descriptions:

1. Verbal Communication	A. Involving body language, facial expressions, gestures, and eye contact.
2. Written Communication	B. Involving spoken words, whether in person, via phone calls, or video chats.
3. Visual Communication	C. Containing emails, letters, reports, and text messages.
4. Non-verbal Communication	D. Utilizing visual aids such as graphs, charts, logos, and videos.

Q2. Match the following communication barriers with their descriptions:

1. Physical Barriers	A. Involving personal elements like stress, anger, or mistrust that impact message delivery and reception.
2. Language Barriers	B. Differences in cultural backgrounds may result in misinterpretations.
3. Psychological Barriers	C. Distance and physical obstacles that can disrupt message transmission.
4. Cultural Barriers	D. Variances in language or vocabulary can lead to misunderstandings.
5. Perceptual Barriers	E. Arising from differences in perception and viewpoints.

CHAPTER 8

MOTIVATION AT WORKPLACE

INTRODUCTION

Workplace motivation is a crucial element that impacts employee performance, job satisfaction, and organizational success. It comprises internal and external factors that drive individuals to achieve goals, perform effectively, and contribute positively.

Kindly answer to all the questions provided at the conclusion of the chapter. This will allow you to assess your comprehension of the topic and determine whether a brief recap or a more thorough reading is necessary.

MASLOW'S HIERARCHY

Motivation in the workplace aligns with Maslow's Hierarchy and we will conclude this chapter with the same. Often visualized as a pyramid featuring five tiers, this model charts the progression of human needs from the most primary to the more intricate (Figure 1). Maslow posited that individuals must fulfil lower-level needs before delving into higher-level growth requirements. This section delves into each level of the hierarchy, offering instances to elucidate how these needs materialize in everyday life.

Basic Physiological Needs

At the foundation of Maslow's hierarchy lie physiological needs, serving as the fundamental prerequisites for human survival. These contain necessities like air, water, sustenance, shelter, garments, and rest. Without meeting these essentials, the human body cannot operate effectively.

Examples:

An individual stranded in a desert giving top priority to locating water and food.

Homeless individuals seeking shelter to shield themselves from severe weather conditions.

A worker taking a break to have lunch, ensuring they possess the energy to efficiently carry out their tasks.

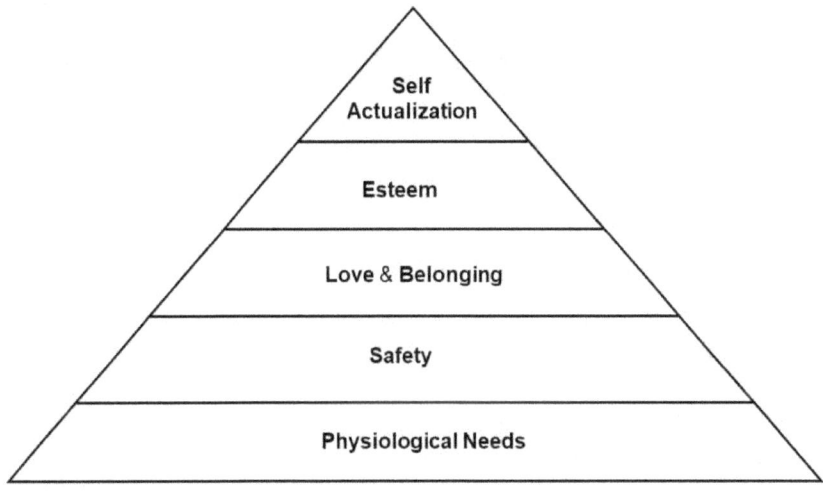

Figure 1 [Maslow's Hierarchy]

Safety Needs

Once physiological needs are satisfied, the subsequent tier focuses on safety and security. This incorporates physical safety, financial stability, health and wellness, and safeguarding against mishaps and maladies.

Examples:

A family installing a home security system to ward off intrusions.

An employee seeking a steady job with health coverage and retirement benefits for long-term security.

Communities constructing robust infrastructures such as fire services and police departments to safeguard residents.

Love And Belongingness Needs

The third level contains social needs. Humans are inherently social beings who yearn for relationships, companionships, and a sense of inclusion. Love, intimacy, and connections with others are vital for psychological well-being.

Examples:

A student joining school clubs and organizations to build friendships and a sense of companionship.

Couples nurturing strong relationships through shared experiences and mutual support.

Individuals engaging in religious or community groups to feel interconnected and valued.

Esteem Needs

Esteem needs are bifurcated into self-esteem (self-respect, accomplishments) and esteem gained from others (appreciation, status). Meeting these needs develops feelings of self-assurance and value.

Examples:

An employee being recognized or promoted for their dedicated efforts.

An artist showcasing their artwork in a gallery, garnering admiration and acknowledgment from the public.

A person setting and attaining personal fitness objectives, culminating in a sense of achievement and self-esteem.

Self-Actualization Needs

At the pinnacle of the hierarchy stands self-actualization, denoting the realization of an individual's potential, self-fulfilment, and personal development. It contains the aspiration to reach one's maximum potential.

Examples:

A musician innovating compositions and continually honing their craft.

An entrepreneur launching a business aligned with their passions and values.

An individual pursuing lifelong learning, perpetually seeking new knowledge and experiences.

INTRINSIC MOTIVATION

Originating from within an individual, intrinsic motivation drives engagement in work due to its inherent interest, enjoyment, or fulfillment. Employees motivated intrinsically demonstrate higher levels of creativity, commitment, and satisfaction. Encouraging factors like meaningful tasks, autonomy, personal growth opportunities, and acknowledgment of accomplishments are vital for cultivating intrinsic motivation.

EXTRINSIC MOTIVATION

Extrinsic motivation relies on external rewards such as salary, bonuses, promotions, and benefits. While effective in motivating employees, over-reliance on extrinsic rewards can lead to short-term compliance rather than enduring commitment. A balanced approach incorporating both intrinsic and extrinsic motivators often yields optimal results.

LEADERSHIP'S INFLUENCE

Effective leadership is instrumental in nurturing a motivated workforce. Leaders who set clear goals, offer constructive feedback, and genuinely care about their employees' well-being substantially increase motivation levels. Leadership styles promoting collaboration, trust, and empowerment tend to create a more motivated and engaged team.

WORK ENVIRONMENT

A positive work environment is essential for sustaining employee motivation, characterized by a supportive culture, professional development opportunities, and a healthy work-life balance. Organizations promoting inclusivity and respect are more likely to retain motivated and high-performing employees.

ACKNOWLEDGMENT AND INCENTIVES

Recognizing and rewarding employees for their contributions can enhance morale and motivation. Recognition may involve verbal praise, awards, or advancement opportunities. Timely and authentic acknowledgment helps employees feel valued and appreciated, reinforcing their dedication to the organization.

CASE STUDY: IMPLEMENTING MASLOW'S HIERARCHY OF NEEDS AT GREENTECH INC.

Background

GreenTech Inc., a mid-sized company focusing on renewable energy, faced challenges related to employee motivation and retention. To tackle these issues, management opted to apply strategies aligned with Maslow's Hierarchy of Needs. The goal was to cultivate a more fulfilling work environment and enhance overall employee contentment.

Physiological Needs

GreenTech prioritized meeting the fundamental physiological needs of its workforce by ensuring a comfortable and well-equipped workplace. This included providing complimentary healthy meals, access to clean drinking water, regular break times, and competitive salaries to help employees cover essential needs.

Safety Needs

The company addressed safety concerns by offering comprehensive health insurance, retirement benefits, and long-term job security. They also invested in a rigorous workplace safety program, containing regular safety exercises and ergonomic office setups. Additionally, security systems were installed to safeguard employees and assets, cultivating a protected work environment.

Love and Belongingness Needs

Recognizing the significance of social connections, GreenTech organized frequent team-building activities and social gatherings. Employees were encouraged to engage in interest-based groups, volunteer in community service initiatives, and participate in a mentorship program designed to cultivate a sense of belonging and support.

Esteem Needs

In an effort to elevate self-esteem and recognition, GreenTech launched an employee recognition program that acknowledged accomplishments and milestones. Employees were recognized and praised publicly for outstanding performance, promoting a culture of appreciation. The company also offered avenues for professional growth, allowing employees to pursue personal development and career progression.

Self-Actualization Needs

GreenTech empowered employees to pursue their passions and introduce innovation within their roles. They provided resources for continuous learning, such as workshops, courses, and conferences. Employees were granted autonomy in their projects and encouraged to contribute ideas aligned with their individual and professional aspirations.

Outcomes

Implementing Maslow's Hierarchy of Needs yielded substantial benefits at GreenTech. There was a noticeable increase in employee morale and job satisfaction, leading to enhanced productivity and creativity. Reduced turnover rates resulted from the sense of security and belonging, while recognition and development opportunities motivated employees to excel. The emphasis on self-actualization nurtured a culture of innovation, positively impacting the company's growth and accomplishments in the renewable energy sector.

Through the comprehensive application of Maslow's Hierarchy of Needs, GreenTech Inc. established an encouraging and inspiring work atmosphere. This case exemplifies how recognizing and fulfilling employees' needs can drive heightened motivation, satisfaction, and organizational triumph.

CONCLUSION

In conclusion, workplace motivation is multifaceted, containing intrinsic and extrinsic elements. By creating a supportive environment, exhibiting effective leadership, and acknowledging employee efforts, organizations can cultivate a motivated and flourishing workforce.

Maslow's Hierarchy of Needs offers a valuable lens into comprehending human motivation and conduct. By acknowledging the diverse strata of needs, individuals and organizations can more effectively address and fulfil them, resulting in more meaningful, satisfying, and productive lives. Understanding this hierarchy enables us to grasp not just our own behaviours and motivations but also those of others, promoting empathy and enhancing communication and support in various contexts.

-------------- Multiple Choice Type Questions --------------

Q1. Who proposed the concept of the Hierarchy of Needs?

A. Sigmund Freud
B. Carl Rogers
C. Abraham Maslow
D. B.F. Skinner

Q2. What lies at the foundation of Maslow's Hierarchy of Needs?

A. Safety Needs
B. Esteem Needs
C. Basic Physiological Needs
D. Self-Actualization Needs

Q3. Which of the following is an example of Safety Needs?

A. A worker taking a break to have lunch
B. A family installing a home security system
C. A student joining school clubs
D. An artist showcasing their artwork

Q4. Love and Belongingness Needs include:

A. Financial stability and health coverage
B. Relationships, companionships, and a sense of inclusion
C. Realization of an individual's potential
D. Fundamental prerequisites for human survival

Q5. Which need is associated with self-respect and accomplishments?

A. Self-Actualization Needs
B. Safety Needs
C. Love and Belongingness Needs
D. Esteem Needs

Q6. Self-Actualization is best exemplified by:

A. A musician innovating compositions
B. A family installing a home security system
C. A worker taking a break to have lunch
D. A student joining school clubs

Q7. Which of the following statements about Maslow's Hierarchy of Needs is true?

A. It is a rigid, linear progression without any fluctuation.
B. Cultural and individual differences can influence the hierarchy.
C. It does not include any physical needs.
D. It is universally accepted without any criticisms.

Q8. Which of the following is a critique of Maslow's Hierarchy of Needs?

A. It captures all intricacies of human motivation.
B. It oversimplifies human motivation.
C. It universally applies without cultural variations.
D. It includes cognitive and aesthetic needs.

Q9. What is the primary impact of workplace motivation on employees?

A. Increased absenteeism
B. Improved job satisfaction
C. Reduced job performance
D. Decreased organizational success

Q10. Which of the following is a characteristic of intrinsic motivation?

A. Driven by external rewards
B. Originates from within an individual
C. Leads to short-term compliance
D. Relies solely on promotions

Q11. What role does effective leadership play in employee motivation?

   A. Increasing job dissatisfaction

   B. Setting unclear goals

   C. Promoting collaboration, trust, and empowerment

   D. Ignoring employee well-being

Q12. How can organizations sustain employee motivation through the work environment?

   A. By offering minimal professional development opportunities

   B. By creating a supportive culture and promoting inclusivity

   C. By disregarding work-life balance

   D. By reducing opportunities for personal growth

-------------------- **Match The Following** --------------------

Q1. Match the examples with the corresponding level of Maslow's Hierarchy of Needs:

1. A worker taking a break to have lunch.	A. Love and Belongingness Needs
2. An artist showcasing their artwork in a gallery.	B. Safety Needs
3. A student joining school clubs and organizations.	C. Basic Physiological Needs
4. A family installing a home security system.	D. Self-Actualization Needs
5. A musician innovating compositions.	E. Esteem Needs

Q2. Match the needs with their descriptions:

1. Self-Actualization Needs	A. Relationships, companionships, and a sense of inclusion.
2. Love and Belongingness Needs	B. Realization of an individual's potential and self-fulfilment.
3. Esteem Needs	C. Fundamental prerequisites for human survival.
4. Safety Needs	D. Physical safety, financial stability, and health.
5. Basic Physiological Needs	E. Self-respect, accomplishments, and appreciation from others.

CHAPTER 9

SIX THINKING HATS

INTRODUCTION

The Six Thinking Hats approach, created by Edward de Bono, a respected consultant, is widely utilized in research, education, and business settings to enhance idea development and decision-making processes while aligning group thinking. This method involves six imaginary hats, each representing a specific thinking style. By "wearing" a hat, individuals engage solely in that mode of thinking, enabling seamless shifts between different perspectives and preventing conflicting viewpoints within a group.

This concept of "thinking hats" simplifies the understanding for participants, as it builds on familiar expressions like "put on your thinking cap." Users can easily switch between hats, promoting diverse thinking rather than being stuck in one mind-set. De Bono crafted this method in response to team deadlock in critical decision-making, aiming to inculcate fresh idea generation and effective problem-solving. The structured nature of the Six Thinking Hats aids groups in overcoming challenges and achieving innovation.

Kindly answer all the questions given at the end of the chapter. This will help you gauge your understanding of the topic and decide if a quick scan or a more detailed reading is needed.

CORE PRINCIPLES OF THE SIX THINKING HATS

De Bono categorized six distinct thinking approaches, assigning each a distinct color for easy recognition and visualization. Each hat contain a specific type of thinking with unique guidelines, ensuring comprehensive discussion and exploration of ideas within a group setting.

Crucially, the Six Thinking Hats method emphasizes behavioural modes over individual personalities, encouraging every participant to engage in diverse thinking styles. This inclusive approach ensures a thorough examination of issues and culminates in well-rounded, consensus-based decisions through open dialogue.

BREAKDOWN OF THE SIX HATS

The White Hat – Factual Analysis

The White Hat focuses on verifiable data and existing information, emphasizing a neutral, fact-based perspective.

The Red Hat – Emotional Insight

The Red Hat allows for the expression of feelings and intuitive responses without the need for justification, capturing emotional reactions effectively.

The Yellow Hat – Positive Thinking

The Yellow Hat promotes optimism by exploring potential benefits, opportunities, and advantages related to the topic at hand.

The Black Hat – Critical Assessment

The Black Hat highlights potential risks, drawbacks, and challenges, offering a critical viewpoint to identify possible pitfalls.

The Green Hat – Creative Solutions

The Green Hat encourages creativity and innovation, promoting the generation of novel ideas and the enhancement of existing concepts, commonly used in brainstorming sessions.

The Blue Hat – Thought Management

The Blue Hat, worn by the discussion leader, oversees the thinking process, sets the agenda, ensures hat adherence, and summarizes discussions and conclusions.

ILLUSTRATIVE SCENARIOS

Achieving Consensus

Reaching a consensus in group decision-making, a key application of the Six Thinking Hats technique, allows for comprehensive exploration of problems and opportunities from various perspectives. This method promotes an inclusive environment where individuals can voice their opinions freely, leading to decisions based on collective insight rather than individual bias.

Creativity and Innovation

Implementing the Six Thinking Hats technique aids teams in selecting innovative ideas from brainstorming sessions for further development. By leveraging each hat's unique function, teams can thoroughly assess creative concepts, facilitating structured thinking and informed decision-making throughout the innovation process.

CASE STUDY

Let's consider the case of Anumita, a new employee at Innovative Softwares (IS) facing challenges during her Initial Learning Program training. With constraints such as travel logistics and accommodation, the Six Thinking Hats method can provide a structured approach to address Anumita's situation.

Application of the Hats to Anumita's Scenario

White Hat: Gather factual details on travel options, IS policies, and constraints.

Red Hat: Consider Anumita's emotions and her family's concerns about the journey.

Yellow Hat: Identify the advantages of different travel choices to ensure convenience and cost-effectiveness.

Black Hat: Evaluate risks associated with each option, including disruptions and accommodation issues.

Green Hat: Generate innovative solutions like a blended travel approach or alternate accommodations for family members.

Blue Hat: Manage the decision-making process, incorporating varied perspectives and summarizing the final plan for implementation.

CONCLUSION

The Six Thinking Hats technique serves as a valuable tool for structuring discussions and decision-making by guiding groups through diverse thinking modes. Breaking away from conventional thought patterns, this method promotes creativity and critical thinking, offering a structured path to optimal solutions in scenarios ranging from consensus-building to addressing complex challenges.

-------------- Multiple Choice Type Questions --------------

Q1. Who created the Six Thinking Hats approach?

A. John Boyd
B. Edward de Bono
C. Robert Kaplan
D. Dr. Paul Hersey

Q2. What is the primary purpose of the Six Thinking Hats method?

A. To improve financial decision-making
B. To enhance idea development and decision-making processes
C. To provide guidelines for physical fitness
D. To teach public speaking skills

Q3. Which hat focuses on verifiable data and existing information?

A. Red Hat
B. Black Hat
C. White Hat
D. Green Hat

Q4. What does the Red Hat represent in the Six Thinking Hats method?

A. Critical assessment
B. Emotional insight
C. Positive thinking
D. Thought management

Q5. Which hat is used for promoting creativity and innovation?

A. Yellow Hat
B. Blue Hat
C. Green Hat
D. White Hat

Q6. What is the function of the Blue Hat in the Six Thinking Hats method?

A. Generating innovative ideas
B. Overseeing the thinking process
C. Emphasizing optimism
D. Expressing emotions

Q7. In the Six Thinking Hats method, which hat focuses on potential risks and challenges?

A. White Hat
B. Red Hat
C. Black Hat
D. Green Hat

Q8. How does the Yellow Hat contribute to the decision-making process?

A. By highlighting potential benefits and opportunities
B. By analysing factual data
C. By managing the overall thinking process
D. By expressing intuitive responses

Q9. What type of thinking does the Six Thinking Hats method emphasize over individual personalities?

A. Emotional thinking
B. Behavioural modes
C. Logical reasoning
D. Creative thinking

Q10. Which hat would be worn by the discussion leader to set the agenda and ensure adherence to the thinking process?

A. Red Hat
B. Yellow Hat
C. Blue Hat
D. Green Hat

------------------- **Match The Following** -------------------

Q1. Match the following Six Thinking Hats with their corresponding functions:

1. White Hat	A. Critical Assessment
2. Red Hat	B. Factual Analysis
3. Yellow Hat	C. Emotional Insight
4. Black Hat	D. Creative Solutions
5. Green Hat	E. Thought Management
6. Blue Hat	F. Positive Thinking

CHAPTER 10

CREATIVITY AND ITS BLOCKS

INTRODUCTION

Innovation plays a critical role in the growth and success of an individual and organizations. Establishing a culture of innovation entails creating an environment that values and nurtures new ideas. This chapter presents essential strategies for encouraging such a culture, including promoting open communication, supporting risk-taking, providing adequate resources, acknowledging creativity, and building diverse teams. It also delves into creative problem solving approaches such as brainstorming, mind mapping and overseeing innovation processes from idea conception to execution. By leveraging these insights, organizations can effectively cultivate and oversee innovation, stimulating continuous improvement and success. Despite the benefits of innovation, individuals often encounter blocks such as resource constraints, fear of failure, and lack of expertise. Create a culture that views failure as a learning opportunity, celebrates attempts, and encourages risk-taking.

Please attempt to all the questions given in the chapter. This will help you evaluate your understanding of the topic and decide if you need a quick refresh or a more comprehensive reading.

CULTURE OF INNOVATION

Creating a culture of innovation in an organization involves promoting an environment where fresh ideas are appreciated and nurtured. Here are some essential strategies for cultivating such a culture.

Encourage Open Communication

Innovation thrives in a setting where employees feel at ease sharing their ideas and feedback. Promote open dialogue and active listening at all levels of the organization.

Support Risk-Taking

Innovation often requires taking risks and exploring uncharted territories. Establish a safe environment where employees can confidently experiment with new ideas without the fear of failure or reprisal.

Provide Resources and Time

Innovation demands resources like time, money, and tools. Allocate dedicated time for brainstorming and creative thinking. Offering access to relevant training and resources can also promote innovative thinking.

Recognize and Reward Creativity

Appreciate and reward employees who contribute innovative ideas. Recognition can come in the form of praise, awards, or incentives, motivating others to think creatively.

Diverse Teams

Assemble diverse teams with varying perspectives, backgrounds, and skills. Diversity often leads to a wider range of ideas and more creative solutions.

Leadership Support

Leaders should exemplify innovative behaviour and actively endorse and support their teams to think creatively. When leaders show a commitment to innovation, it sets the tone for the whole organization.

CREATIVE PROBLEM-SOLVING TECHNIQUES

Effective problem-solving is vital for innovation. Here are some techniques to enhance creativity in problem-solving.

Brainstorming

This classic technique involves generating numerous ideas within a short period. Encourage participants to build on each other's ideas and refrain from criticism during the brainstorming session.

Mind Mapping

Create a visual representation of ideas related to a central problem. This helps in organizing thoughts, identifying relationships, and revealing new connections.

SCAMPER

SCAMPER stands for Substitute, Combine, Adapt, Modify, Put to another use, Eliminate and Rearrange. This acronym prompts different ways of thinking about and solving problems by considering various modifications to existing ideas or products.

Six Thinking Hats

Developed by Edward de Bono, this technique involves looking at a problem from six different perspectives, each represented by a different colored hat, facilitating comprehensive thinking. This is discussed in detail in a separate chapter.

Role Playing

Acting out scenarios and considering different viewpoints by putting oneself in another person's shoes can lead to fresh insights and ideas, aiding in creative problem-solving.

Random Word Association

Use a randomly chosen word to spark new ideas related to a problem, leading to unexpected connections and innovative solutions.

MANAGING INNOVATION PROCESSES

Effectively managing the innovation process is essential for translating creative ideas into tangible outcomes. Here are steps to manage innovation processes.

Idea Generation

Gather a wide range of ideas from various sources, encouraging input from employees, customers, and stakeholders through brainstorming sessions, suggestion boxes, and surveys.

Idea Evaluation

Evaluate ideas based on criteria like feasibility, potential impact, cost, and alignment with organizational goals. Select the most promising ideas for further development.

Prototyping and Testing

Develop prototypes or pilot versions of selected ideas, testing them in real-world conditions to refine ideas and enhance their success.

Implementation

Develop a detailed implementation plan once an idea is refined, including resource allocation, task assignment, and timelines, with effective project management being crucial.

Monitoring and Evaluation

Monitor progress post-implementation, gathering feedback to assess impact and effectiveness and making necessary adjustments based on feedback.

Continuous Improvement

Encourage continuous improvement by regularly reviewing and updating processes, incorporating feedback, and staying open to new ideas.

BLOCKS TO CREATIVITY

Numerous fears tend to limit their actions to safe endeavours, potentially hindering the full realization of their capabilities. This can result in the development of issues such as stereotyping, overlooking available resources, and dulling of sensibilities. Conversely, individuals facing these limitations may experience self-doubt in unfamiliar situations, leading to fears of failure, uncertainty, embarrassment, and social disapproval. Numerous common obstacles hinder divergent thinking and the creative process, making it imperative to address the following blocks to cultivate a creative mind-set.

Fear of Failure

Since childhood, an exaggerated fear of failure may have developed due to the tendency to reward success and penalize failure. Individuals harbouring such fears often shy away from challenges and risks. Embracing failure as an integral part of life is crucial for overcoming this obstacle, as it provides valuable insights and growth opportunities. Adopting a perspective that views failure as a stepping stone for learning encourages experimentation and promotes innovation.

Allergy to Ambiguity

Many individuals find ambiguity, uncertainty, or complexity unsettling, with some individuals displaying a heightened aversion to such situations. Preferring structure and order, these individuals tend to avoid ambiguous scenarios, limiting their potential for growth and creativity. Confronting ambiguity can lead to a sense of satisfaction from problem-solving and unravelling complexities. Viewing complex situations as challenges, rather than insurmountable puzzles, can help dissolve this block.

Sensitivity

Fear of humiliation and rejection can impede collaboration with others, making it challenging for touchy individuals to seek help or form connections. This behaviour often stems from fragile self-esteem. Overcoming sensitivity involves realistically assessing one's strengths and weaknesses, recognizing the necessity of constructive criticism for personal development. Developing a robust self-concept independent of external opinions is essential for promoting collaboration and engaging in creative endeavours.

Conformity

While conformity offers a sense of security by maintaining the status quo, it stifles innovation, which propogates on change and fresh perspectives. Challenging conventions and habitual behaviours through exposure to diverse cultures and recognizing and rewarding creative efforts can help break free from conformity.

Resource Myopia

Many individuals fail to recognize the resources at their disposal, known as resource myopia. By cultivating curiosity about one's environment and actively seeking available resources, individuals can enhance their problem-solving skills and stimulate creativity by leveraging their strengths and available resources effectively.

Starved Sensibilities

The demands of modern life can dampen our capacity for imagination and emotions, referred to as starved sensibility. This condition may result from an overemphasis on specialized knowledge and societal pressures favouring rationality over creativity. Reviving our senses and emotions is crucial for nurturing divergent thinking and creativity. Cultivating an interest in the arts, nature, science, sports, literature, engaging hobbies, and creating friendships with individuals receptive to new ideas can help reignite neglected sensibilities.

Rigidity

Rigidity, characterized by resistance to adaptability, presents a common impediment to creativity. This manifests in the form of stereotypes, closed-mindedness, and functional fixedness, limiting our ability to perceive uniqueness and embrace innovation. Overcoming rigidity entails making a conscious effort to eschew stereotypes, develop a mind-set of open-mindedness, and explore alternative applications for objects and ideas.

CASE STUDY 1: NURTURING AN INNOVATIVE CULTURE AT TECH SOLUTIONS INC.

Context

At Tech Solutions Inc., a company in the middle of the technology industry, there was a need to break out of a cycle of limited product growth and market expansion. Acknowledging the importance of innovation, the leadership decided to reshape the company's culture to spark creativity and fresh concepts. Guiding this transformation was CEO Radha, who recognized that innovation is fundamental to maintaining a competitive edge.

Situation

Radha's first step was to promote transparent communication across the organization. She urged employees at every level to freely share their ideas, setting up forums and regular brainstorming sessions. Radha ensured that feedback was respected and taken into account, developing a culture where everyone's voice was heard.

Realizing that innovation often involves taking risks, Radha created a safe space for experimentation. She reassured employees that failure was a natural part of learning and not something to fear. This shift in perspective empowered employees to explore new ideas without the dread of negative consequences.

Approaches to Encouraging Innovation

Allocation of Resources: Radha dedicated specific time and resources to innovation. Weekly "innovation hours" enabled employees to concentrate solely on creative thinking and idea generation. She also offered access to training programs to enhance creative skills.

Acknowledgment and Incentives: Radha established a rewards system for innovative ideas. Employees who contributed valuable ideas were acknowledged in company meetings and received financial incentives and accolades. This motivated other to actively engage in creative thinking.

Diverse Teams: Radha assembled diverse teams with members from varied backgrounds, skillsets, and viewpoints. This diversity resulted in a broader range of ideas and more innovative problem-solving solutions.

Support from Leadership: Radha and the leadership team led by example, showcasing their dedication to innovation. They actively engaged in brainstorming sessions and backed innovative projects, setting a precedent that reverberated throughout the organization.

Execution and Results

Tech Solutions Inc. adopted creative problem-solving methods such as brainstorming and mind mapping to address challenges. Techniques like the SCAMPER method and role-playing were integrated into regular team activities, enhancing creative problem-solving approaches.

To manage the innovation process effectively, Radha introduced structured phases: idea generation, assessment, prototyping, and execution. Ideas were assessed based on feasibility and potential impact, with the most promising ones progressing to prototyping and testing.

In a year, Tech Solutions Inc. experienced significant advancements. The new culture of innovation resulted in the creation of three new products, boosting market share and customer satisfaction. Employee morale and engagement also rose, as the lively and inclusive atmosphere made them feel appreciated and inspired. This case study exemplifies how cultivating an innovative culture, employing creative problem-solving techniques, and overseeing the innovation process can propel organizational progress and achievement.

CASE STUDY 2: OVERCOMING BLOCKS TO CREATIVITY AT INNOVATETECH CORP

Background

InnovateTech Corp, a leading technology firm, prided itself on innovation but noticed a decline in creative output. The company's management realized that employees faced numerous blocks to creativity, impacting their ability to generate innovative ideas. The CEO, Esha, initiated a comprehensive program to address these blocks and develop a culture of creativity.

Scenario

Esha started by identifying common obstacles hindering creativity at InnovateTech. Employees expressed fears of failure and ambiguity, sensitivity to criticism, conformity to established norms, resource myopia, starved sensibilities, and rigidity in thinking. Esha and her team devised strategies to tackle each block systematically.

Strategies for Overcoming Blocks

Fear of Failure: To address the fear of failure, Esha implemented a "Fail Fast, Learn Fast" initiative. This program encouraged employees to experiment and learn from their mistakes without fear of repercussions. Failure was reframed as a valuable learning experience, and success stories of innovative projects born from initial failures were shared across the company.

Allergy to Ambiguity: Esha introduced ambiguity training workshops, helping employees develop comfort with uncertainty. These workshops included problem-solving exercises that required navigating ambiguous situations, promoting a mindset that views complexity as an opportunity rather than a challenge.

Sensitivity: To reduce sensitivity to criticism, Esha promoted a culture of constructive feedback. Regular peer review sessions were established, where feedback was given in a supportive and developmental context. Employees were trained to give and receive feedback positively, focusing on growth and improvement.

Conformity to Norms: Esha encouraged diversity and inclusivity by forming cross-functional teams. Exposure to different perspectives and ideas was facilitated through cultural exchange programs and creative thinking workshops. Employees were rewarded for challenging the status quo and bringing fresh ideas to the table.

Resource Myopia: To combat resource myopia, Esha launched a "Resource Awareness" campaign. Employees were trained to identify and leverage available resources effectively. Internal resource directories and knowledge-sharing platforms were created to enhance accessibility to tools, information, and expertise.

Starved Sensibilities: Esha promoted engagement with arts, nature, and other creative activities. InnovateTech hosted regular events like art exhibitions, nature walks, and creative writing workshops, encouraging employees to revive their senses and emotions, thus stimulating divergent thinking.

Rigidity: Esha addressed rigidity by encouraging open-mindedness and flexibility. Employees participated in brainstorming sessions where stereotypes and fixed notions were challenged. Innovation labs were set up to experiment with new ideas and applications, creating an environment of continuous learning and adaptation.

Outcome: Within a year, InnovateTech Corp experienced a significant boost in creative output and innovation. The blocks to creativity were effectively addressed, leading to a more dynamic and innovative workplace. Employee morale improved, and the company saw the successful launch of several ground breaking products. This case study underscores the importance of systematically addressing creativity blocks to unlock an organization's full innovative potential.

CONCLUSION

Innovation and creativity play crucial roles in the growth and success of any organization. By inculcating a culture of innovation, utilizing creative problem-solving techniques, effectively managing innovation processes, and overcoming blocks, organizations can leverage new ideas to drive progress and maintain competitiveness. Embracing innovation not only leads to better products and services but also cultivates a dynamic and engaging workplace where employees feel valued and motivated to contribute their best. Blocks to creativity, including fears and limitations, perpetuate a cycle that stifles creative endeavours. To disrupt this cycle, it is imperative to address and overcome these blocks, creating an environment conducive to innovative thinking and problem-solving. By doing so, individuals and communities can unlock their creative potential and thrive in a rapidly evolving world.

-------------- Multiple Choice Type Questions --------------

Q1. What is the first step in managing the innovation process?

A. Idea Evaluation

B. Implementation

C. Idea Generation

D. Monitoring and Evaluation

Q2. Which creative problem-solving technique involves generating numerous ideas within a short period?

A. Mind Mapping

B. Role Playing

C. Brainstorming

D. Random Word Association

Q3. What does SCAMPER stand for in creative problem-solving?
   A. Substitute, Combine, Adapt, Modify, Put to another use, Eliminate, Rearrange
   B. Simplify, Combine, Adjust, Modify, Plan, Execute, Review
   C. Select, Combine, Analyse, Modify, Plan, Evaluate, Reinvent
   D. Substitute, Compare, Adjust, Modify, Place, Evaluate, Reorganize

Q4. Which strategy involves promoting open dialogue and active listening at all levels of the organization?
   A. Provide Resources and Time
   B. Encourage Open Communication
   C. Support Risk-Taking
   D. Recognize and Reward Creativity

Q5. What does the "Six Thinking Hats" technique entail?
   A. Looking at a problem from six different perspectives
   B. Using six random words to generate ideas
   C. Creating a visual map of six ideas
   D. Combining six different brainstorming sessions

Q6. What is essential for overcoming blocks to innovation in organizations?
   A. Reducing the number of brainstorming sessions
   B. Securing funding and allocating dedicated time for innovation
   C. Limiting the number of team members in innovation projects
   D. Implementing strict guidelines for idea generation

Q7. Which factor is NOT mentioned as a block to innovation?
   A. Resource constraints
   B. Fear of failure
   C. Lack of expertise
   D. Excessive diversity

Q8. What role does leadership play in realising a culture of innovation?
   A. Leaders should exemplify innovative behaviour and actively endorse creative thinking
   B. Leaders should minimize their involvement to let employees take full control
   C. Leaders should only support ideas that have immediate financial benefits
   D. Leaders should focus on maintaining traditional practices

Q9. What is a crucial element in creativity, involving the generation of new ideas or combining known elements in novel ways?
A. Memory recall
B. Analogical thinking
C. Cognitive functions
D. All of the above

Q10. Which of the following blocks is characterized by individuals avoiding risks due to an exaggerated fear of failing, often developed from childhood?
A. Allergy to Ambiguity
B. Fear of Failure
C. Sensitivity
D. Conformity to Norms

Q11. What is the term for individuals failing to recognize the resources at their disposal?
A. Starved Sensibilities
B. Resource Myopia
C. Rigidity
D. Perceptual Blocks

Q12. Which block involves acknowledging failure as a learning experience and viewing complex situations as growth opportunities?
A. Engaging in various activities
B. Realistically assessing strengths and weaknesses
C. Confronting fears
D. Challenging conventions

Q13. Which block describes the modern life's demands that dampen imagination and emotions, reducing divergent thinking?
A. Resource Myopia
B. Sensitivity
C. Starved Sensibilities
D. Rigidity

Q14. What is the impact of fear of humiliation and rejection on creativity?

    A. It leads to resource myopia.

    B. It impedes collaboration and seeking help.

    C. It promotes innovative thinking.

    D. It promotes an open-minded approach.

Q15. Which block to creativity involves resistance to adaptability, stereotypes, and closed-mindedness?

    A. Conformity to Norms

    B. Sensitivity

    C. Rigidity

    D. Allergy to Ambiguity

Q16. What does reviving senses and emotions through activities such as arts, nature, and literature help overcome?

    A. Resource Myopia

    B. Fear of Failure

    C. Starved Sensibilities

    D. Sensitivity

-------------------- **Match The Following** --------------------

Q1. Match the following creative problem-solving techniques with their descriptions:

1. Brainstorming	A. Looking at a problem from six different perspectives.
2. Mind Mapping	B. Generating numerous ideas within a short period without criticism.
3. SCAMPER	C. Acting out scenarios and considering different viewpoints.
4. Six Thinking Hats	D. Using a randomly chosen word to spark new ideas.
5. Role Playing	E. Considering various modifications to existing ideas or products.
6. Random Word Association	F. Creating a visual representation of ideas related to a central problem.

Q2. Match the following strategies for realising a culture of innovation with their descriptions:

1. Encourage Open Communication	A. Establish a safe environment where employees can confidently experiment with new ideas.
2. Support Risk-Taking	B. Promote open dialogue and active listening at all levels of the organization.
3. Provide Resources and Time	C. Appreciate and reward employees who contribute innovative ideas.
4. Recognize and Reward Creativity	D. Allocate dedicated time for brainstorming and creative thinking.
5. Diverse Teams	E. Assemble teams with varying perspectives, backgrounds, and skills.
6. Leadership Support	F. Leaders should exemplify innovative behaviour and actively endorse creative thinking.

Q3. Match the following blocks to creativity with their descriptions:

1. Fear of Failure	A. Fear of humiliation and rejection hinders collaboration and seeking help.
2. Allergy to Ambiguity	B. Maintaining the status quo offers security but stifles innovation and fresh perspectives.
3. Sensitivity	C. Failing to recognize and utilize available resources effectively.
4. Conformity to Norms	D. People with low tolerance for uncertainty prefer structure and avoid complex situations.
5. Resource Myopia	E. Modern life's demands dampen imagination and emotions, reducing divergent thinking.
6. Starved Sensibilities	F. Individuals avoid risks due to an exaggerated fear of failing, stemming from childhood.
7. Rigidity	G. Resistance to adaptability, stereotypes, and closed-mindedness limit creativity.

PART 2

ORGANIZATIONAL MANAGEMENT

CHAPTER 11

CONFLICT MANAGEMENT

INTRODUCTION

Conflict arises when the interests of two individuals seem to clash. In such cases, one's actions can be understood in terms of two main aspects: assertiveness and cooperativeness. Assertiveness measures how much a person focuses on addressing their own needs, while cooperativeness examines how much they consider the needs of others.

Please take a moment to answer all the questions at the end of the chapter. This will help you gauge your understanding of the subject and decide whether you need a quick review or a deeper study.

CONFLICT MODES

The Thomas Kilmann Conflict Model evaluates a person's actions using two dimensions, outlining five approaches to handling conflict: Competing, Collaborating, Compromising, Avoiding, and Accommodating (Figure 1). Each method differs in assertiveness and cooperativeness, offering diverse strategies for resolving conflicts.

COMPETING

Competing involves assertiveness and uncooperativeness. It is a power-driven approach where a person prioritizes their own interests, often at the cost of others, and employs various power tactics to secure their stance. This can involve advocating for one's rights, upholding a position, or striving to emerge victorious.

Signs of Overuse

Constant tension: Over use of this style can be exhibited through constant tension and outburst of violent temper.

Fear of admitting ignorance: In a competitive setting, individuals may display more confidence than they truly possess, inhibiting both learning and transparency.

Signs of Underuse

Feeling powerless: Underutilizing competition may suggest a lack of awareness or unease with exercising power, which can restrict one's impact.

Trouble taking a stand: Concern for others' emotions or unease about wielding authority can result in uncertainty, which can then potentially create additional problems.

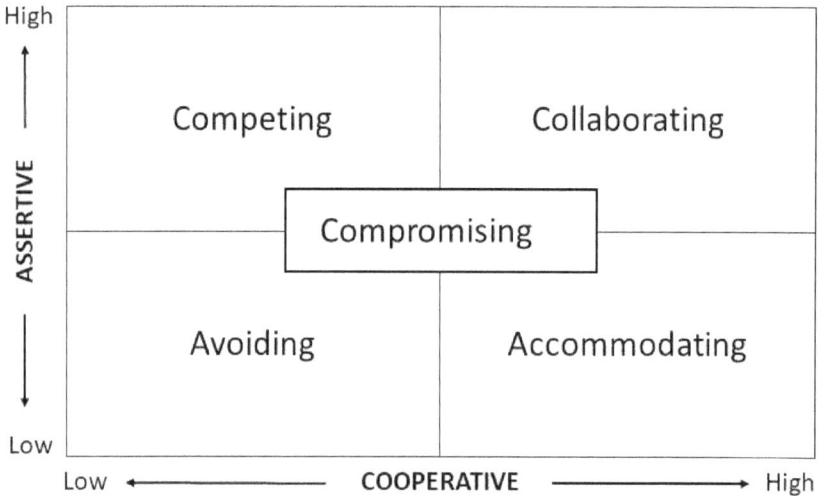

Figure 1 [Conflict Management Approaches]

COLLABORATING

Collaborating requires both assertiveness and cooperation. It entails partnering with others to discover a resolution that entirely addresses the interests of both sides. This approach delves into the problem to pinpoint fundamental issues and explores options that fulfil the needs of all parties involved.

Signs of Overuse

Over-discussing trivial issues: Collaborating takes time and energy, and using it excessively for minor issues can deplete resources.

Failing to elicit collaborative responses: Trust and transparency might be overlooked by others, resulting in overlooking signs of defensiveness or conflicting interests.

Signs of Underuse

Viewing differences pessimistically: Failure to acknowledge the opportunity for shared gains in disputes may hinder you from reaping mutual advantages.

Lack of commitment from others: Failure to address others' concerns in decisions may lead to their lack of commitment.

COMPROMISING

Compromising involves a moderate level of assertiveness and cooperativeness. The objective is to discover a mutually agreeable solution that partly meets the needs of both sides. It falls between competition and accommodation, involving more concession than competition but less than accommodation, and tackling the problem more directly than avoidance but less thoroughly than collaboration.

Signs of Overuse

Overemphasis on tactics: Focusing excessively on the practical aspects of compromise may result in unintentional compromises on principles or long-term goals.

Creating a cynical climate: Excessive negotiations may erode trust and divert focus from the essential matters.

Signs of Underuse

Reluctance to bargain: Being sensitive or embarrassed can hinder fair negotiations, reducing one's effectiveness.

Difficulty making concessions: Conflicts can escalate without compromise, resulting in mutually destructive arguments.

AVOIDING

Avoidance is characterized as being passively uninvolved and uncooperative. When engaging in avoidance, a person abstains from addressing their own interests or the interests of others. This approach may include tactfully evading a matter, deferring it, or removing oneself from a daunting predicament.

Signs of Overuse

Coordination issues: Avoidance on crucial matters can impede coordination.

Atmosphere of caution: Excessive avoidance may result in creating an atmosphere where problems are left unattended, ultimately leading to unresolved conflicts.

Signs of Underuse

Hurting others' feelings: Lack of prudence and diplomacy can provoke conflicts.

Feeling overwhelmed: Failure to establish priorities can lead to feeling overwhelmed by a multitude of issues.

ACCOMMODATING

Accommodation is characterized by being passive and willing to cooperate. This approach entails putting aside one's own needs in order to address the needs of others, sometimes involving sacrificing personal interests. It can manifest as generous acts without expecting anything in return, following instructions unquestioningly, or accepting others' opinions.

Signs of Overuse

Neglecting personal concerns: Overly accommodating may lead to a loss of influence and recognition, as well as undervaluing your contributions within the organization.

Lack of discipline: Not enforcing essential rules and procedures can potentially damage the organization.

Signs of Underuse

Trouble building goodwill: Ignoring minor concerns that are important to others can impede the process of building relationships.

Being viewed as unreasonable: Rigidly following rules without taking legitimate exceptions into account can lead to avoidable conflict.

CASE STUDY: CONFLICT MANAGEMENT STRATEGIES IN THE WORKPLACE

Context

XYZ Corporation, a mid-sized tech company, is known for promoting a collaborative work culture. However, with company growth, conflicts arose among team members, particularly within the marketing department. These conflicts often stemmed from differences in opinions on project priorities, resource allocation, and individual responsibilities.

Situation

Within the marketing team, there was growing tension between two members, Paritosh and Ananya. Paritosh, known for his assertiveness, often led with his ideas while expecting compliance. Ananya, on the other hand, leaned towards cooperation and accommodated others' requests at times, affecting her workload. A conflict emerged between them regarding the direction of a new marketing campaign.

Applied conflict resolution approaches:

Competing (Paritosh's Approach): Paritosh pushed for an aggressive campaign strategy, aiming to launch ahead of competitors, dismissing Ananya's concerns.

Overuse Indicators:

Surrounding himself with constant tension.

Creating an environment where team members fear admitting gaps in knowledge.

Accommodating (Ananya's Approach): Ananya initially agreed with Paritosh to avoid conflict, neglecting her own concerns and suggestions.

Overuse Indicators:

Neglecting personal views, leading to frustration and burnout.

Decrease in influence within the team due to excessive accommodation.

Steps towards Resolution

Anna intervened by guiding Paritosh and Ananya to adapt varying conflict-handling modes based on the context.

Collaborating: Anna facilitated a team meeting to encourage open discussions, considering both Paritosh and Ananya's viewpoints. They delved into the campaign's core issues, devising a plan merging Paritosh's assertiveness with Ananya's caution.

Result: A well-rounded campaign plan balancing risk and competitiveness to satisfy both.

Compromising: Anna helped Paritosh and Ananya find middle ground, agreeing to trial the aggressive strategy in a smaller market before full implementation.

Result: Testing the strategy gradually to minimize risk exposure before a widespread launch.

Avoiding: Identifying minor issues between Paritosh and Ananya, Anna deferred resolution, focusing on urgent matters and enhancing team coordination.

Result: Reduced immediate tensions and prevented minor issues from escalating.

Accommodating: Anna advised Paritosh to consider Ananya's suggestions for project success, enhancing team cohesion.

Result: Increased morale for Ananya and showcased Paritosh's cooperative spirit, strengthening team unity. Effective use of varied conflict-handling modes by Anna successfully resolved the conflict between Paritosh and Ananya. This experience underscored the significance of employing diverse conflict resolution strategies for harmonious teamwork, ultimately leading to enhanced strategies and a positive work environment.

CONCLUSION

There are various approaches to handling conflicts, and each approach has its own value in different situations, showcasing valuable social skills. All five conflict-handling modes have their place: "Collaborating" emphasizes teamwork, "Accommodating" focuses on goodwill, "Compromising" aims for middle ground, "Avoiding" promotes peace, and "Competing" highlights assertiveness. The effectiveness of each mode depends on the context and the skill used in applying it. Individuals can utilize all five conflict-handling modes, even though they may lean towards certain ones due to personal preference and proficiency. Conflict resolution methods are influenced by both personal tendencies and the circumstances at hand. Becoming adept in all five modes can improve one's conflict management abilities, ensuring more successful and amicable interactions.

-------------- Multiple Choice Type Questions --------------

Q1. What are the two main aspects of a person's actions when conflict arises?

A. Assertiveness and cooperativeness
B. Authority and flexibility
C. Power and influence
D. Competitiveness and passivity

Q2. Which conflict-handling mode involves assertiveness and uncooperativeness?

A. Collaborating
B. Compromising
C. Competing
D. Accommodating

Q3. What is a sign of overuse in the competing mode?

A. Coordination issues
B. Creating a cynical climate
C. Constant tension
D. Failing to elicit collaborative responses

Q4. Which conflict-handling mode requires both assertiveness and cooperation?

A. Avoiding
B. Compromising
C. Collaborating
D. Accommodating

Q5. A sign of underuse in the compromising mode is:

A. Coordination issues
B. Over-discussing trivial issues
C. Reluctance to bargain
D. Neglecting personal concerns

Q6. Which conflict-handling mode is characterized by being passively uninvolved and uncooperative?

A. Avoiding
B. Compromising
C. Accommodating
D. Collaborating

Q7. What can be a result of overusing the accommodating mode?

A. Creating an atmosphere of caution
B. Overemphasis on tactics
C. Neglecting personal concerns
D. Surrounded by "yes" people

Q8. Which conflict-handling mode is associated with moderate levels of assertiveness and cooperativeness?

A. Avoiding
B. Competing
C. Compromising
D. Collaborating

--------------------- **Match The Following** ---------------------

Q1. Match the following conflict-handling modes with their characteristics:

1. Competing	A. Combines assertiveness and cooperation, seeking a resolution that fully satisfies both parties' interests.
2. Collaborating	B. Involves assertiveness and uncooperativeness, prioritizing one's own interests at the expense of others.
3. Compromising	C. Passively uninvolved and uncooperative, avoiding addressing the interests of oneself or others.
4. Avoiding	D. Moderately assertive and cooperative, seeking a mutually agreeable solution that partially satisfies both parties.
5. Accommodating	E. Passive and cooperative, putting aside one's own needs to address the needs of others.

CHAPTER 12

TEAM DYNAMICS

INTRODUCTION

In any professional environment or project scenario, comprehending team dynamics is fundamental for achieving success. Teams consist of individuals with diverse roles, duties and their interactions significantly impact their performance and efficiency. This chapter delves into team roles, responsibilities, performance, effectiveness, and different team models to assist you in navigating the intricacies of working within a team.

Please answer all the questions provided in the chapter. This will enable you to assess your grasp of the topic and determine whether you need a quick review or a deeper study.

TEAM ROLES AND RESPONSIBILITIES

Each team member fulfils a distinct role and carries specific responsibilities, which may vary based on the project requirements. Here are some typical team roles.

Leader

Leaders offer guidance, motivation, and direction to the team, making decisions, setting objectives, and ensuring alignment towards common goals.

Coordinator

Coordinators organize and delegate tasks, ensuring equitable distribution of work among team members and promoting communication and collaboration.

Contributor

Contributors are accountable for completing particular tasks or deliverables, utilizing their skills and expertise to contribute to project success.

Facilitator

Facilitators aid in conflict resolution, promote teamwork, and ensure seamless operation of meetings, promoting a positive and inclusive team environment.

Specialist

Specialists possess specialized knowledge or skills crucial for the project, offering expertise in fields like technology, design, or finance.

Evaluator

Evaluators monitor the team's progress, identify strengths and weaknesses, and provide feedback for enhancement, facilitating the team's learning and growth.

Understanding and fulfilling these roles and responsibilities enables team members to collaborate more efficiently and attain superior outcomes.

TEAM PERFORMANCE AND EFFECTIVENESS

Team performance refers to the collective output and achievements of the team as a whole, while effectiveness gauges how well the team attains its goals. Several factors influence team performance and effectiveness:

Communication

Clear and open communication is essential for collaboration and coordination, preventing misunderstandings and ensuring alignment.

Collaboration

Effective collaboration involves leveraging strengths and skills to work collectively towards a shared goal, enhancing productivity.

Conflict Resolution

Managing conflict constructively is vital for maintaining team harmony and optimizing performance.

Decision Making

Effective decision-making considers diverse perspectives, weighing options to reach informed, timely decisions aligned with team goals.

Feedback and Reflection

Regular feedback and reflection aid in identifying areas for improvement, ensuring continuous team growth through learning from both successes and failures.

TEAM MODELS

Enhancing team dynamics to achieve optimal performance is paramount. Various team models offer frameworks for analyzing and improving team functionality. Here are three well-known models, detailed with examples:

Tuckman's Stages of Group Development

Tuckman's Stages of Group Development is a model outlining the phases teams experience as they come together and grow. The stages include:

Forming: Team members acquaint themselves and grasp the team's goals.

Storming: Conflicts arise as individual's express opinions and compete for roles.

Norming: The team establishes norms, resolves conflicts, and develops cohesion.

Performing: The team efficiently works towards achieving its objectives.

Adjourning: The team disbands after reaching its goals.

Example

Imagine a project team assigned to develop a new software application.

Forming: Team members introduce themselves, share backgrounds, and discuss the project scope.

Storming: Disagreements arise over design choices and task assignments, challenging collaboration.

Norming: Through facilitated discussions and team-building activities, roles are clarified, and a working agreement is reached.

Performing: Smoothly operating, the team meets milestones and collaborates effectively.

Adjourning: Post successful application launch, the team celebrates and disbands.

Belbin's Team Roles

Belbin's Team Roles model identifies nine roles individuals may play in a team based on their behavioral strengths and weaknesses. The roles are as follow.

Plant: Creative problem solver with innovative ideas.

Resource Investigator: Outgoing team member who explores opportunities.

Coordinator: Delegates tasks and promotes decision-making.

Shaper: Challenges the team to improve and meet standards.

Monitor Evaluator: Analytical thinker who critically evaluates strategies.

Teamworker: Diplomatic team player who collaborates effectively.

Implementer: Turns concepts into practical actions.

Completer Finisher: Detail-oriented individual ensuring quality.

Specialist: Brings in-depth knowledge to the team.

Example

Consider a marketing team strategizing a new campaign.

Plant: Generates innovative ideas for the campaign.

Resource Investigator: Explores networking opportunities for resources and partnerships.

Coordinator: Organizes meetings and ensures inclusive decision-making.

Shaper: Challenges the team to meet deadlines and maintain progress.

Monitor Evaluator: Critically evaluates campaign strategies and outcomes.

Teamworker: Mediates conflicts and enhances collaboration.

Implementer: Develops a detailed plan and timeline for campaign execution.

Completer Finisher: Ensures precision and quality in all campaign materials.

Specialist: Provides expertise in digital marketing tactics.

The Five Dysfunctions of a Team

The Five Dysfunctions of a Team model, by Patrick Lencioni, identifies common obstacles hindering team performance and offers strategies to overcome them.

Absence of Trust: Reluctance to be vulnerable hinders team support.

Fear of Conflict: Avoiding productive conflict stalls progress.

Lack of Commitment: Unclear goals lead to inconsistent efforts.

Avoidance of Accountability: Failure to hold each other responsible diminishes performance.

Inattention to Results: Personal goals overshadow team success.

Example

Imagine a sales team struggling to achieve targets.

Absence of Trust: Reluctance to share challenges leads to inadequate support.

Fear of Conflict: Unaddressed issues cause hidden tensions.

Lack of Commitment: Unclear goals result in inconsistent efforts towards targets.

Avoidance of Accountability: Mediocrity arises from unaddressed poor performance.

Inattention to Results: Team success is overshadowed by individual goals and egos.

Solution

Building Trust: Through team-building activities and open communication, trust develops.

Encouraging Conflict: Constructive expression of differing opinions is encouraged.

Clarifying Goals: Setting clear, achievable objectives ensures commitment.

Establishing Accountability: Regular check-ins and reviews enforce accountability.

Focusing on Results: Prioritizing team success aligns individual achievements with team goals.

Understanding and applying these models helps teams navigate dynamics effectively, promoting improved collaboration and performance.

CONCLUSION

Understanding team behaviour, roles, responsibilities, performance, and various models enhances effectiveness as a team member or leader. Effective teams serve as the cornerstone of successful projects and organizations, necessitating investment in understanding and optimizing team dynamics for long-term success.

------------- **Multiple Choice Type Questions** -------------

Q1. What is the primary focus on Exploring Team Dynamics?

A) Understanding team roles and responsibilities
B) Enhancing team communication
C) Optimizing team performance
D) Exploring various team models

Q2. Which team role involves offering guidance, motivation, and direction to the team?

A) Coordinator
B) Contributor
C) Facilitator
D) Leader

Q3. What does Tuckman's Stages of Group Development describe?

A) Team communication patterns
B) Phases of team formation
C) Team performance metrics
D) Conflict resolution strategies

Q4. Which team model identifies nine team roles based on individuals' behavioural traits?

A) Tuckman's Stages of Group Development
B) Belbin's Team Roles
C) The Five Dysfunctions of a Team
D) Herzberg's Two-Factor Theory

Q5. What is essential for maintaining team harmony and optimizing performance?

A) Collaboration
B) Conflict Resolution
C) Feedback and Reflection
D) Decision Making

Q6. What is a common factor influencing team effectiveness according to the text?

A) Team Roles and Responsibilities
B) Communication
C) Collaboration
D) Team Models

-------------------- **Match The Following** --------------------

Q1. Match the following concepts related to Exploring Team Dynamics with their descriptions:

1. Team Performance	A. Describes the phases of team formation, guiding teams through challenges like forming, storming, norming, performing, and adjourning.
2. Team Roles	B. Identifies nine team roles based on individuals' behavioural traits, ensuring a balanced distribution for improved productivity and cohesion.
3. Team Models	C. Refers to leveraging strengths and skills to work collectively towards a shared goal, enhancing productivity.
4. Communication	D. Essential for collaboration and coordination, preventing misunderstandings and ensuring alignment.
5. Collaboration	E. Managing conflict constructively is vital for maintaining team harmony and optimizing performance.
6. Conflict Resolution	F. Effective decision-making considers diverse perspectives, weighing options to reach informed, timely decisions aligned with team goals.
7. Decision Making	G. Regular feedback and reflection aid in identifying areas for improvement, ensuring continuous team growth.
8. Feedback and Reflection	H. Refers to the collective output and achievements of the team as a whole, while effectiveness gauges how well the team attains its goals.

CHAPTER 13

TRANSACTIONAL ANALYSIS

INTRODUCTION

Transactional Analysis (TA), a psychoanalytic theory developed by psychiatrist Eric Berne in the late 1950s, revolutionized Freud's concept of the human psyche. Berne proposed three ego states: The Parent, Adult, and Child states shaped by childhood experiences. Unhealthy childhood experiences can damage these ego states, leading to discomfort or mental illness. By analysing interactions and ego states, TA aims to promote personal improvement. Berne identified social interactions as "games" and published his theories in widely-read books, making TA accessible to many therapists. In 1964, Berne devoted TA purists founded the International Transactional Analysis Association (ITAA), establishing TA as a credible research and professional entity.

Kindly answer all the questions given at the end of the chapter. This will help you evaluate your understanding of the subject and decide if you need a quick refresh or a more comprehensive review.

OUTLINE OF TRANSACTIONAL ANALYSIS

TA serves as both a personality theory and psychotherapy for personal growth. It includes a theory of personality, communication, child development, psychopathology, therapeutic application, and various educational and organizational uses.

THE EGO-STATE (PARENT-ADULT-CHILD, PAC) MODEL

TA, like Neuro-linguistic Programming (NLP), is pragmatic in seeking practical solutions. The PAC Model delineates the Parent, Adult, and Child ego states, each influencing behaviour based on past experiences. These ego states can become contaminated, leading to misconceptions and dysfunctional behaviour.

TRANSACTIONS AND STROKES

Transactions represent communication flow, containing explicit and psychological levels. Strokes, positive or negative responses from others, influence behaviour based on past experiences.

Examples

Positive Strokes:

I really appreciate you being in my life.

You did an excellent job on that project.

Negative Strokes:

You are a terrible person.

You messed up this report.

KINDS OF TRANSACTIONS

Interactions occur when both individuals respond to the ego state of the other person.

Examples

Adult to Adult: "Have you finished writing the report?" "Yes, I'm just about to send it to you."

Child to Child: "Do you want to watch a movie together?" "I'd love to - what should we watch?"

Parent to Child: "Is your room tidy yet?" "Stop bothering me! I'll get to it eventually!"

CROSSED TRANSACTIONS

These occur when individuals address ego states different from those of their partners, leading to communication breakdowns.

Examples

Adult to Adult: "Have you finished working on that report?" "Stop nagging me! I'll get to it."

Parent to Child: "Have you tidied your room?" "I'm going to do it, actually."

DUPLEX OR COVERT TRANSACTIONS

These involve simultaneous implicit psychological transactions alongside explicit social conversations.

Example: "Would you like to visit the barn?" "I've loved barns since I was young." (Social level adult-to-adult; psychological level child-to-child flirtation).

REDEFINING AND DISCOUNTING

Redefining: This entails distorting reality to fit one's preferred view. For example, someone with a "struggling alone against a harsh world" mentality may see kindness as manipulation.

Discounting: Undervaluing something, resulting in responses that do not address the real issue or ignoring evidence to the contrary. This can lead to passivity, agitation, or even anger and violence.

INJUNCTIONS AND DRIVERS

Transactional Analysis identifies common life script injunctions like "Don't be yourself," countered by childhood 'drivers' like "Be perfect" or "Try hard," shaping behaviour and influencing responses.

CASE STUDY:

IMPLEMENTING TRANSACTIONAL ANALYSIS AT INNOVATIVE SOLUTIONS CORP.

Overview

Innovative Solutions Corp., a technology company, encountered internal communication obstacles and interpersonal conflicts among its staff. In response, the management decided to tackle these challenges using TA to enhance understanding and interactions within the team. Collaborating with a

TA-trained consultant, the company aimed to nurture better communication and resolve underlying conflicts.

Initial Evaluation

The consultant conducted a preliminary assessment to pinpoint prevalent ego states and common transactional patterns among employees. It was evident that numerous interactions were marked by crossed and duplex transactions, resulting in misunderstandings and tension. For instance, during a team meeting, a manager's Adult-to-Adult inquiry, "Have you completed the project report?" was defensively met with a Child-to-Parent response, "Stop pressuring me! I'll finish it."

Application of the PAC Model

To tackle these issues, the consultant introduced the Parent-Adult-Child (PAC) model to the team. Employees were briefed on the three ego states:

Parent: Reflecting behaviors and attitudes acquired from authority figures.

Adult: Offering logical, objective, and data-oriented responses.

Child: Expressing emotions, creativity, and spontaneity based on past experiences.

Through workshops and role-playing scenarios, employees practiced recognizing their own and others' ego states during interactions and adapting their responses for more effective communication. For example, the defensive employee was coached to respond from an Adult ego state, acknowledging the manager's query with composure, "I'm on track to finish it by the deadline."

Handling Crossed and Covert Transactions

Staff members were trained to identify and rectify crossed transactions that often led to communication breakdowns. In one instance, an Adult-to-Adult question from a team member, "Can we discuss the project details?" received an unexpected Parent-to-Child response, "I don't have time for this right now." Recognizing the crossed transaction, the consultant guided the respondent to rephrase their response from an Adult perspective: "Let's schedule a specific time to discuss this in detail."

The concept of duplex or covert transactions was also highlighted, where implicit messages complicated explicit communications. Employees learned to align their social and psychological messages to prevent misinterpretations.

Addressing Redefining and Discounting

The consultant tackled common issues of redefining and discounting among team members. For instance, one employee perceived constructive feedback as personal criticism due to a life script of "struggling alone against a harsh world." This employee was coached to acknowledge and challenge this redefinition, viewing feedback as a growth tool rather than a personal affront.

Similarly, discounting behaviors, like undervaluing one's contributions, were recognized and corrected. Employees were taught to appreciate their achievements and respond appropriately to compliments and positive feedback.

Injunctions and Drivers

The consultant guided employees in recognizing and overcoming negative injunctions and drivers influencing their conduct. For example, an employee with the injunction "Don't be yourself" and the driver "Be perfect" was encouraged to embrace authenticity and self-acceptance, leading to enhanced self-esteem and interpersonal connections.

Outcomes

The implementation of TA at Innovative Solutions Corp. resulted in notable enhancements in communication and team dynamics. Staff members became more skilled at recognizing and adjusting their ego states, reducing conflicts and improved collaboration. The deeper understanding of transactional patterns and ego states created a more supportive and productive work atmosphere.

Transactional Analysis offered Innovative Solutions Corp. a thorough framework for addressing communication challenges and interpersonal disputes. By grasping and applying the PAC model, recognizing crossed and duplex transactions, and addressing redefining and discounting behaviours, the company established a healthier and more efficient organizational culture. This case study illustrates the practical application of TA in a corporate context, showcasing its potential for personal development and enhancing professional interactions.

CONCLUSION

Transactional Analysis suggests that people are fundamentally okay and capable of adult thinking, shaping their fate through decisions that are open to change. Overcoming maladaptive childhood scripts is crucial for autonomy, spontaneity, intimacy, and effective problem-solving. TA prioritizes healing over mere progress, promoting new choices and personal growth.

Berne's skill in communicating TA concepts in everyday language contributed to its widespread appeal, albeit with some oversimplifications. Harris's "I'm OK, You're OK" differs from fundamental TA beliefs, reflecting distinctions in life position perspectives.

Overall, TA offers a comprehensive framework for understanding personality, communication, and growth, serving as valuable tools in therapy, education, and organizational analysis.

-------------- **Multiple Choice Type Questions** --------------

Q1. Who developed Transactional Analysis (TA) as a psychoanalytic theory?

A. Carl Jung
B. Sigmund Freud
C. Eric Berne
D. Albert Ellis

Q2. What are the three ego states proposed by Eric Berne in TA?

A. Adult, Child, and Adolescent
B. Parent, Child, and Adolescent
C. Parent, Adult, and Child
D. Parent, Adult, and Adolescent

Q3. What does the Parent-Adult-Child (PAC) Model in TA represent?

A. Different personality types
B. Three stages of human development
C. Three ego states influencing behaviour
D. Communication styles

Q4. What are strokes in Transactional Analysis?

A. Positive responses from others
B. Negative responses from others
C. Positive or Negative responses from others
D. Types of transactions

Q5. Which type of transaction occurs when individuals address ego states different from those of their partners?

A. Reciprocal or Complementary Transactions
B. Crossed Transactions
C. Duplex or Covert Transactions
D. Injunctions and Drivers

Q.6 What is one characteristic of Duplex or Covert Transactions in TA?

A. They involve simultaneous explicit social conversations only.
B. They occur when both individuals respond to each other's ego states.
C. They include implicit psychological transactions alongside explicit social conversations.
D. They lead to communication breakdowns.

Q7. What does Redefining entail in Transactional Analysis?

A. Distorting reality to fit one's preferred view.
B. Undervaluing something, leading to inappropriate responses.
C. Countering childhood 'drivers' with life script injunctions.
D. Involving communication interactions where both individuals respond to each other's ego states.

Q8. What is one key idea emphasized in Transactional Analysis?

A. People are fundamentally flawed.

B. People are fundamentally okay and capable of adult thinking.

C. People's behaviours are solely shaped by external factors.

D. People's childhood experiences do not influence their adulthood.

-------------------- **Match The Following** --------------------

Q1. Match the following concepts in Transactional Analysis with their descriptions:

1. Reciprocal or Complementary Transactions	A. Distorting reality to fit one's preferred view.
2. Crossed Transactions	B. Common life script injunctions countered by childhood 'drivers.'
3. Duplex or Covert Transactions	C. Communication interactions where both individuals respond to each other's ego states.
4. Redefining	D. Simultaneous implicit psychological transactions alongside explicit social conversations.
5. Discounting	E. Undervaluing something, leading to inappropriate responses or ignoring evidence.
6. Injunctions and Drivers	F. Addressing ego states different from those of the partners, causing communication breakdowns.

CHAPTER 14

JOHARI'S WINDOW

INTRODUCTION

Johari's Window, a psychological tool developed in 1955 by psychologists Joseph Luft and Harry Ingham, combines their first names to form the unique moniker "Johari." This model serves as a valuable instrument for individuals to gain insights into their relationships with both themselves and others, promoting self-awareness and mutual understanding within various social dynamics.

Please ensure to respond to all the questions provided at the conclusion of the chapter. This will assist you in assessing your comprehension of the topic and determining if you require a brief revision or a more in-depth study.

THE FOUR QUADRANTS OF JOHARI'S WINDOW

It comprises four distinct quadrants, each delineating different facets of self-awareness and interpersonal communication. They are Open Area, Blind Area, Hidden Area and Unknown Area as shown in Figure 1.

Open Area (Arena)

The open area signifies elements known both to the individual and to others. It contains behaviors, attitudes, skills, and experiences that are openly shared and mutually recognized.

Example: Imagine a team leader, Lakshmi, renowned for her exceptional organizational skills. Acknowledging her strengths, she openly exhibits proficiency in project management. Her colleagues appreciate and are aware of these capabilities. During meetings, Lakshmi takes the lead in task organization and deadline setting, actions recognized and valued by everyone.

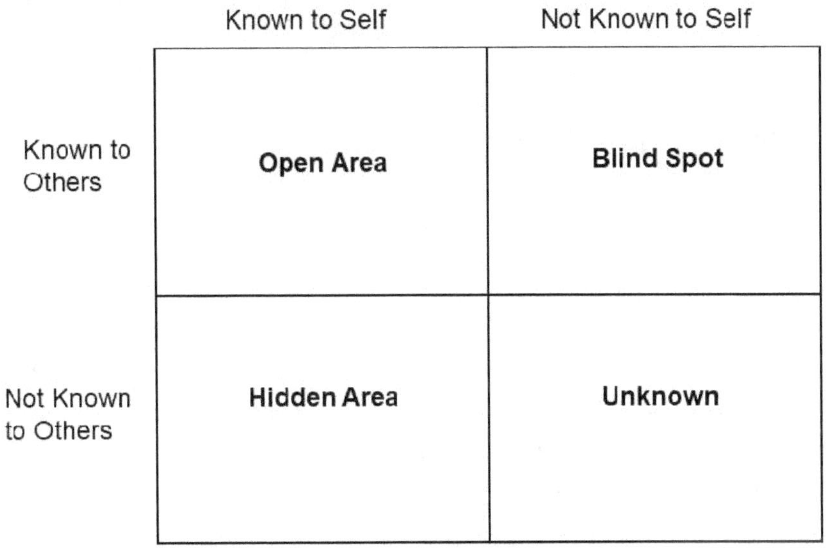

	Known to Self	Not Known to Self
Known to Others	**Open Area**	**Blind Spot**
Not Known to Others	**Hidden Area**	**Unknown**

Figure 1 [Johari's Window]

Blind Area (Blind Spot)

The blind area contains aspects of an individual perceived by others but not acknowledged by the individual themselves. It can include habits, behaviours, or attitudes visible to others but unseen by oneself.

Example: Rakesh is a diligent worker but has a habit of unintentionally interrupting others during meetings. His colleagues find this disruptive, though Krishna remains oblivious to this behaviour. During a feedback session, his peers highlight this tendency. Initially surprised, Krishna reflects on the feedback and starts monitoring his behaviour, gradually reducing interruptions.

Hidden Area (Façade)

The hidden area consists of personal information known to the individual but concealed from others. This sphere may comprise personal fears, secrets, or experiences that one opts not to disclose.

Example: Alka excels in public speaking but experiences anxiety with each presentation. Despite her anxiety, she conceals it well, leading her colleagues to perceive her as confident and unfazed. Alka fears that unveiling her anxiety might tarnish her perceived competence. Over time, as she establishes trust within her team, she shares her feelings, receiving support and reassurance that aids in better managing her anxiety.

Unknown Area (Unknown)

The unknown area comprises aspects of the self-unbeknownst to both the individual and others. This realm may harbour latent abilities, subconscious sentiments, or untapped potential awaiting discovery.

Example: Krishna, accustomed to a career in finance, remains unexplored in creative writing. Attending a workshop out of curiosity, he uncovers a hidden talent for storytelling. Neither Krishna nor his colleagues were cognizant of this aptitude. Delving deeper into writing, he unearths a newfound passion, infusing creativity into his professional endeavours, surprising both himself and his peers.

EXPANDING THE OPEN AREA

The central aim of Johari's Window utilization is to expand the open area, nurturing improved communication and robust relationships. This objective can be realized through:

Self-Disclosure: Sharing more personal information to transition data from the hidden area to the open area.

Feedback: Receiving constructive input to reduce the blind area by acknowledging unknown behaviours or attitudes.

Discovery: Engaging in new activities and experiences to uncover unknown realms, promoting self-awareness and personal growth.

PRACTICAL APPLICATIONS

In the Workplace

Leveraging Johari's Window within team contexts can elevate collaboration and trust. Teams can conduct routine feedback sessions where members provide constructive insights regarding each other's strengths and areas for enhancement. This practice enhances individual awareness of blind spots and transparent communication.

Example: A marketing team integrates Johari's Window into a team-building retreat. Each member completes a self-assessment and receives peer feedback. Through this exercise, they unveil hidden talents and blind spots among team members. Discovering Jane's innovative skills despite her reserved nature, the team encourages her to share more, leading to innovative marketing endeavours.

In Personal Development

Individuals can employ Johari's Window to enrich self-awareness and personal development. By soliciting feedback from acquaintances or colleagues, they can uncover blind spots and comprehend how they are perceived by others.

Example: Emma, an aspiring leader, solicits feedback from her mentor concerning her communication style. Discovering an unintentional tendency to appear overly critical, Emma works on her delivery, becoming more attuned to her tone and approach. This refinement aids in promoting better relationships within her team.

CONCLUSION

Johari's Window stands as a potent framework for advancing self-awareness and interpersonal relationships. Active involvement in self-disclosure, feedback acquisition, and exploration of novel experiences enables individuals and teams to expand their open areas, nurturing a receptive, supportive, and productive environment. Embracing this model can cultivate heightened communication, deeper connections, and personal and professional advancement.

-------------- **Multiple Choice Type Questions** --------------

Q1. Who developed Johari's Window?

A. Abraham Maslow and Carl Rogers
B. Sigmund Freud and Carl Jung
C. Joseph Luft and Harry Ingham
D. B.F. Skinner and Krishna Watson

Q2. What is the primary purpose of Johari's Window?

A. To assess cognitive abilities
B. To promote self-awareness and mutual understanding
C. To measure emotional intelligence
D. To develop leadership skills

Q3. Which quadrant represents behaviors known both to the individual and to others?

A. Blind Area
B. Hidden Area
C. Open Area
D. Unknown Area

Q4. In Johari's Window, the 'Blind Area' includes:

A. Personal fears and secrets not shared with others
B. Aspects of an individual that are unknown to both the individual and others
C. Habits or behaviors that others can see but the individual cannot
D. Skills and experiences openly shared and recognized by others

Q5. Which activity can help expand the 'Open Area' by transitioning information from the hidden area?

A. Self-Disclosure
B. Avoidance
C. Competition
D. Meditation

Q6. How can one reduce the 'Blind Area'?

A. Through self-reflection
B. By engaging in new activities
C. By soliciting feedback
D. Through solitary meditation

-------------------- **Match The Following** ---------------------

Q1. Match the Johari's Window Quadrant with its description:

1. Open Area (Arena)	A. Aspects known to the individual but hidden from others.
2. Blind Area (Blind Spot)	B. Aspects known to both the individual and others.
3. Hidden Area (Façade)	C. Aspects unknown to both the individual and others.
4. Unknown Area (Unknown)	D. Aspects perceived by others but unknown to the individual.

CHAPTER 15

COMPETENCY MAPPING

INTRODUCTION

Competencies can be defined as observable performance, the standard or quality of a person's performance outcomes, or the underlying attributes of an individual, and often involve a combination of these elements. One perspective emphasizes the actual performance of an individual, including their output and tasks completed. These performances are regarded as competencies that can be demonstrated, observed, and evaluated to earn recognition as competent. Another viewpoint considers competency as a benchmark or level of quality in results, which can enhance productivity and efficiency in a work environment. A third aspect of competency pertains to the inherent characteristics of an individual, containing their knowledge, skills, and abilities. This definition underscores the importance of individuals' essential inputs for delivering competent performances.

Make sure to attempt to answer all the questions given at the end in the chapter. Doing so will help you evaluate your understanding of the subject matter and decide if a quick scan or a more detailed reading is needed.

COMPETENCY APPPROACHES

There are three main approaches to defining competencies: the educational approach, the psychological approach, and the organizational/business approach. The educational approach concentrates on skill development, meeting standards, and granting certifications. It relies on functional role analysis to define competencies, outlining role outcomes or the knowledge, skills, and attitudes necessary for role performance. These competencies are evaluated against behavioural standards. The psychological approach, which involves behavioural repertoires, posits that personal competencies can be characterized as motives and personality traits that can be identified and imparted to others by observing exceptional performers. These competencies consist of a broad set of knowledge, motives, traits, self-perceptions, social roles, and skills that contribute to superior job performance. The notion of core competencies as the "collective learning" of an organization has gained significant attention and plays a key role in the contemporary discourse on competencies.

COMPETENCY TYPOLOGIES

Competencies can be defined across three key dimensions: generic versus organization-specific, operational versus managerial, and skills versus behaviours.

Generic vs. Organization-Specific Competencies

Generic Competency Templates: Identify common competencies that span various organizations and job roles. These include skills like organizing work, collaborating in a team, and adhering to rules and procedures. These templates are usually tailored to specific industries or designed to meet professional standards and certifications. However, a limitation of generic competencies is their assumption of consistent responsibilities and requisite competencies across organizations, which is not always the case. Similar roles in different companies may entail different levels of requirements and duties.

Organization-Specific Competencies: Developed through methodologies that involve extensive interviews, on-site observations, and document analysis within a particular organization. The primary goal is to create a competency model that aligns with the organization's strategic objectives, aiding in translating strategy into operational terms.

Managerial vs. Operational Competencies

Managerial competencies comprise all managerial duties and can be categorized into five key areas: planning, organizing, controlling, motivating, and coordinating. These competencies may be general, applicable to any managerial role, or specific to an organization, involving self-management and relationship management.

Operational competencies are tied to a particular job with minimal or no managerial responsibilities. They may be specific to an organization, outlining the skills necessary for an employee to align with the enterprise's mission, strategy, and objectives. However, emphasis on operational competencies alone does not enhance overall performance or support an organizational culture focused on maximizing human resources. Therefore, most competency management systems prioritize managerial competencies over operational ones. Nonetheless, when transitioning from task-oriented to competency-based approaches, establishing operational competencies based on job descriptions can serve as a crucial initial phase that is relatively straightforward to achieve and implement within organizations.

Competencies as Skills vs. Competencies as Behaviours

Competencies as skills indicate the level of proficiency in carrying out a specific job, whether operational or managerial. They center on the tasks individuals perform in their roles and are particularly effective in knowledge-based work environments. These skills embody the human element of organizational practices and standard operations, what is known in academic circles as transactional competencies.

Competencies as behaviours, on the other hand, outline the preferred conduct during job execution, emphasizing the manner in which individuals perform their tasks. They serve to define and assess personal behaviour traits such as creativity, initiative, problem-solving persistence, discipline, assertiveness, and empathy. Behavioural competencies can be described as innate abilities and characteristics that define an individual and can be applied irrespective of the specific job or organization. These competencies empower an organization to evolve, challenge existing routines, and alter procedures, thereby facilitating effective change. Behavioural competencies are interlinked with transformational competencies and are increasingly vital in the current organizational landscape characterized by constant upheavals.

COMPETENCY MAPPING

Competency mapping is the process of an individual or organization identifying and outlining the key competencies necessary for success in a work role or situation. This involves recognizing the specific competencies needed to effectively carry out a job or set of tasks. The process entails deconstructing a role or job into its essential tasks or activities, and pinpointing the required competencies (technical, managerial, behavioural, conceptual knowledge, attitude, and skills) for successful performance. A competency map is a compilation of an individual's competencies highlighting the most crucial factors for success in particular jobs, departments, organizations, or industries relevant to the individual's current career path.

COMPETENCY PROFILE

Defining Competency and Formation of Dictionary

Defining competencies for every level or role necessitates recognizing various dimensions that commonly comprise the intensity of actions, size of impact, complexity, degree of effect, unique elements, and level of innovation. Competency dictionaries offer a precise explanation of competencies in technical and behavioural terms along with a series of behavioural cues and a rating scale for each.

The Behavioural Event Interviewing (BEI) technique can be utilized for creating the dictionary by conducting interviews with high-performing employees to pinpoint the competencies that lead to their success.

Explanation of Meta Competency Level

BEI technique can be utilized to establish the dictionary by interviewing successful employees to recognize the competencies that lead to their achievement.

Defining the Matrix of Employee Bands

The BEI technique can be utilized for constructing the dictionary by interviewing accomplished employees to recognize the competencies that lead to their success.

Building a Technical Competency Dictionary

This dictionary generally stems from the organizational functions and the expected roles for carrying out those functions.

Agreeing on the Assessment Set

The assessment set comprises behavioural and technical competencies, bands, levels of matrix, role types, and proficiency benchmarks.

Defining Behavioural Skill Parameters

Behavioural skills need further elaboration immediately following the agreement or identification of competencies. Subsequently, every potential behaviour is comprehensively enumerated and described to clarify behaviour in terms that are observable, understandable, interpretable, and evaluable. Key observable behavioural aspects contain the depth and breadth of knowledge, quality of work produced, provision of guidance and supervision to ensure high-quality outcomes, timeliness in delivering results in specific scenarios, demonstration of leadership, and exhibits of innovation. Behavioural cues are established.

Preparing Assessment Worksheets

Each individual in a role provides a comprehensive description of their behaviour relative to the competencies they are being assessed on. This is then aligned with the job criteria.

Mapping Individual Competencies to Benchmarks and Self-Assessment

The worksheets are aligned with proficiency levels and customized to reflect differences from the defined benchmark for that specific competency in the given role. A comparative analysis is conducted to assess the existing and target positions.

CASE STUDY: ENFORCING COMPETENCY MAPPING AT XYZ CORPORATION

Context

XYZ Corporation, a prominent manufacturing entity, encountered issues related to inconsistent performance within its various departments and job positions. The primary goals were to boost productivity, align employee skills with company objectives, and promote a culture of ongoing enhancement. To tackle these challenges, XYZ Corporation opted to implement competency mapping.

Execution

Under the guidance of the Chief Human Resources Officer (CHRO), the HR department launched an extensive project on competency mapping. The initiative commenced with the delineation of competencies through three distinct approaches: educational, psychological, and organizational. The educational aspect concentrated on skill development and meeting industry benchmarks, the psychological facet highlighted personal competencies like motives and personality characteristics, while the organizational perspective stressed aligning competencies with strategic aims.

Types of Competencies

A distinction was made between generic competencies, applicable industry-wide such as teamwork and adherence to protocols, and organization-specific competencies. The latter were crafted through interviews, observations, and document scrutiny within XYZ Corporation to ensure harmony with strategic goals.

Both managerial and operational competencies were pinpointed. Managerial competencies contained planning, organizing, and motivating, whereas operational competencies were role-specific with fewer managerial duties. A balanced emphasis was placed on both competency types to ensure comprehensive performance improvement.

Competency Mapping Process

The competency mapping process comprised several stages:

Defining Competencies and Creating a Dictionary: A competency dictionary was constructed using the Behavioural Event Interviewing (BEI) method involving interviews with high-performing staff to identify key competencies.

Establishing a Technical Competency Dictionary: This was crafted based on organizational functions and anticipated roles.

Setting Assessment and Behavioural Skill Parameters: Agreement on behavioural and technical competencies was reached, and observable behaviour parameters were defined.

Assessment Worksheets: Employees provided detailed behaviour descriptions relative to competencies, which were then benchmarked against job requirements.

Mapping Individual Competencies: Self-assessments were aligned with proficiency benchmarks to spot gaps and areas for enhancement.

Results: The adoption of competency mapping at XYZ Corporation yielded notable improvements. Recruitment and selection processes were refined, ensuring suitable matches for each position. Performance management systems (PMS) were strengthened with clear performance assessment benchmarks. Tailored training and development sessions targeted competency gaps, leading to enhanced skill levels and job contentment. Compensation management was also synched with competencies, motivating employees to develop requisite skills.

The competency mapping initiative propelled XYZ Corporation into a high-performing entity. By methodically pinpointing and nurturing crucial competencies, the company ensured employees were well-prepared to fulfil their roles effectively and contribute meaningfully to organizational goals. This case study underscores the pivotal role of competency mapping in elevating organizational performance, cultivating a culture of constant improvement and progress.

CONCLUSION

Competency mapping has a significant impact on various HRM subsystems, such as recruitment and selection, performance management systems (PMS), training and development, and compensation management. Implementing a competency-based HRM system leads to the development of a high-performing organization. By methodically identifying and cultivating competencies essential for success, organizations can ensure that their employees are adequately prepared to meet the requirements of their positions and contribute effectively to the organization's objectives. Thus, competency mapping plays a pivotal role in enhancing organizational performance and promoting a culture of continuous improvement and growth.

-------------- **Multiple Choice Type Questions** --------------

Q1. What is the primary focus of the educational approach to defining competencies?

  A. Skill development and meeting standards
  B. Identifying personal motives and personality traits
  C. Enhancing productivity and efficiency
  D. Recognizing the collective learning of an organization

Q2. Which approach to defining competencies involves behavioural repertoires?

  A. Educational approach
  B. Psychological approach
  C. Organizational/business approach
  D. Functional role analysis approach

Q3. What is a limitation of generic competencies?

  A. They are not based on interviews and observations.
  B. They assume consistent responsibilities across organizations.
  C. They do not include behavioural standards.
  D. They focus only on managerial roles.

Q4. Which type of competency is specific to an organization and aligns with its strategic objectives?

  A. Generic Competencies
  B. Operational Competencies
  C. Managerial Competencies
  D. Organization-Specific Competencies

Q5. Operational competencies are primarily tied to:

A. Managerial responsibilities
B. Strategic objectives of an organization
C. Specific job roles with minimal managerial duties
D. Enhancing overall performance and promoting organizational culture

Q6. Competencies as behaviours focus on:

A. The proficiency in carrying out a specific job
B. The tasks performed in roles
C. The manner in which tasks are performed
D. Knowledge-based work environments

Q7. What is the first step in the methodology for preparing a competency profile?

A. Defining the matrix of employee bands
B. Building a technical competency dictionary
C. Defining competency and forming a dictionary
D. Agreeing on the assessment set

Q8. Competency mapping significantly impacts various HRM subsystems. Which of the following is NOT one of them?

A. Recruitment and selection
B. Compensation management
C. Marketing strategy
D. Performance management systems

-------------------- **Match The Following** --------------------

Q1. Match the following competency mapping elements with their descriptions:

1. Competency Dictionary	A. Comprehensive description of behaviour relative to competencies being assessed.
2. Behavioural Event Interviewing (BEI)	B. Precise explanation of competencies in technical and behavioural terms.
3. Assessment Worksheets	C. Technique used for creating competency dictionaries by interviewing high-performing employees.
4. Meta Competency Level	D. High-level competencies identified through successful employee interviews.

Q2. Match the following competency types with their characteristics:

1. Generic Competency Templates	A. Competencies that outline the skills necessary for an employee to align with the enterprise's mission, strategy, and objectives.
2. Managerial Competencies	B. Competencies that define preferred conduct during job execution.
3. Operational Competencies	C. Competencies that are applicable across various organizations and job roles.
4. Behavioural Competencies	D. Competencies containing planning, organizing, controlling, motivating, and coordinating.

CHAPTER 16

LEADING AND MANAGING

INTRODUCTION

In any organization, effective leadership and management are vital for achieving success. While often used interchangeably, these concepts have distinct focuses and functions. Understanding various leadership styles, the dynamics of power and influence, the difference between leadership and management, and strategies for developing leadership skills can empower individuals to be more adept leaders and managers. This chapter delves into these topics using clear and direct language.

Please respond to all the questions provided at the conclusion of the chapter. This will assist you in assessing your comprehension of the topic and determining if you require a brief revision or a more in-depth study.

STYLES OF LEADERSHIP

Leadership styles refer to how leaders guide, motivate, and oversee their teams. Here are some common styles:

Authoritative Leadership

Authoritative leaders make decisions independently without seeking input from others. They expect compliance and offer clear directives. This style can be effective in emergencies but may hinder creativity and diminish morale over time.

Participative Leadership

Participative leaders engage team members in the decision-making process. They value input and encourage collaboration. While this style enhances morale and stimulates creative solutions, it may slow down decision-making.

Transformational Leadership

Transformational leaders inspire and motivate their teams by articulating a compelling vision and leading by example. They focus on overarching goals and encourage innovation. This style can result in high levels of engagement and productivity.

Transactional Leadership

Transactional leaders concentrate on routine tasks and utilize rewards and penalties to manage performance. They prioritize short-term goals and clearly defined structures. While effective for achieving specific objectives, this style may not inspire long-term commitment.

Servant Leadership

Servant leaders prioritize the needs of their team members and concentrate on serving others. They cultivate a supportive and inclusive environment, which can strengthen team cohesion and morale.

Each leadership style has its strengths and is suited to different circumstances. Effective leaders often adjust their style based on their team's needs and the challenges they encounter.

POWER AND INFLUENCE

Power and influence are critical components of leadership, enabling leaders to guide their teams and attain objectives. The primary types of power include:

Positional Power

Positional power originates from an individual's role or title within an organization, granting them the authority to make decisions and allocate resources. For instance, a manager wields positional power due to their job title.

Expert Power

Expert power stems from an individual's skills, knowledge, and expertise. Those with expert power are esteemed for their capabilities and are frequently sought for advice and direction.

Referent Power

Referent power arises from personal traits and relationships. Charismatic and likeable individuals can sway others due to their admired qualities.

Coercive Power

Coercive power involves the capacity to enforce consequences or punishments. Leaders wielding coercive power can influence behaviour through threats or penalties, though this approach may lead to resentment and decreased morale.

Reward Power

Reward power is based on the ability to dispense rewards, such as bonuses, promotions, or recognition. This type of power motivates team members by acknowledging and rewarding their accomplishments.

Effective leaders comprehend how to judiciously employ various types of power to influence and inspire their teams.

LEADERSHIP VS. MANAGEMENT

Although closely linked, leadership and management serve distinct roles:

Leadership

Leadership revolves around envisioning, motivating, and inspiring individuals while driving change. Leaders focus on influencing people, cultivating relationships, and promoting innovation. They consider long-term goals and the big picture.

Management

Management entails planning, organizing, and coordinating resources to achieve specific objectives. Managers concentrate on tasks, processes, and efficiency, ensuring that daily operations run smoothly and short-term goals are accomplished.

Essentially, leadership pertains to people and vision, whereas management pertains to processes and tasks. Both are indispensable for organizational prosperity. A proficient leader can also serve as a competent manager, and vice versa, albeit the skills and emphasis required for each role vary.

DEVELOPING LEADERSHIP SKILLS

Leadership skills can be honed and refined over time through intentional effort and practice. Here are some strategies:

Self-Reflection

Deliberate on your strengths, weaknesses, values, and leadership goals. Self-awareness is the initial step toward enhancing your leadership capabilities.

Solicit Feedback

Regularly seek feedback from peers, mentors, and team members. Constructive criticism offers valuable insights into areas where you can improve.

Continuous Learning

Engage in ongoing learning by reading books, attending workshops, and participating in training programs to explore diverse leadership theories and practices.

Cultivate Empathy

Empathy involves understanding and sharing others' feelings. Developing empathy inculcates stronger relationships and enhances your leadership effectiveness.

Develop Relationships

Invest time in cultivating and nurturing robust relationships with your team members. Trust and respect are critical facets of effective leadership.

Embrace Challenges

Embrace opportunities to lead in varied settings, whether through new projects, roles, or volunteer endeavours. Challenges facilitate personal growth and the development of new skills.

Mentorship

Engage a mentor who can provide guidance and assistance as you enhance your leadership capacities. A mentor offers valuable perspectives stemming from their experience.

By focusing on these strategies, you can elevate your leadership skills and evolve into a more impactful and successful leader and manager.

CASE STUDY: LEADERSHIP AND MANAGEMENT IN A NON-PROFIT ORGANIZATION

Background

Do Good Foundation, a non-profit organization committed to providing education and healthcare services to underprivileged communities, has experienced substantial growth in recent years. As the organization expands, it encounters new leadership and management challenges. To effectively address these challenges, it is essential to grasp different leadership styles, power dynamics, and the distinction between leadership and management.

Scenario

Anumita, the Executive Director of Do Good Foundation, is recognized for her transformational leadership style. She has effectively motivated her team by presenting a compelling vision for expanding their outreach programs. However, with the organization's growth, Anumita has acknowledged the importance of harmonizing her visionary leadership with efficient management practices to ensure operational smoothness and achieve long-term objectives.

Leadership Styles in Action

Transformational Leadership (Anumita's Approach): Anumita communicates a distinct and inspiring vision for Do Good Foundation, concentrating on broadening their educational initiatives to reach more communities. She inspires her team by setting an example and promoting innovation.

Outcome: Team members exhibit high levels of engagement and productivity, feeling motivated and aligned with the organization's objectives.

Participative Leadership: Anumita engages her team in decision-making processes, esteeming their input and promoting collaboration. She conducts regular meetings to discuss new initiatives and gather feedback.

Outcome: Improved morale and innovative solutions, albeit with occasional delays in decision-making due to the necessity for consensus.

Power and Influence

Positional Power: Anumita utilizes her role as Executive Director to make strategic decisions and allocate resources efficiently. She employs her authority to steer the organization towards its mission.

Outcome: Clear directives and well-defined structures ensure the organization's operations run smoothly.

Expert Power: Dr. Krishna, the Head of Medical Programs, wields expert power owing to his extensive knowledge and experience in healthcare. His expertise is sought for advice and direction on medical initiatives.

Outcome: Dr. Krishna's guidance plays a crucial role in shaping effective healthcare programs, earning respect and trust from the team.

Referent Power: Anumita's charismatic and approachable demeanor endears her to the team, enabling her to influence others through personal connections.

Outcome: Strong team cohesion and high morale due to team members being motivated by Anumita's likable qualities.

Leadership vs. Management

Leadership (Anumita's Focus): Anumita emphasizes envisioning and inspiring her team, driving change, and doing innovation. She concentrates on long-term goals and the bigger picture.

Outcome: The team is motivated and aligned with the organization's vision, though operational details may at times be overlooked.

Management (Priyesh's Focus): Priyesh, the Operations Manager, focuses on planning, organizing, and coordinating resources to achieve specific objectives. He ensures smooth daily operations and accomplishes short-term goals.

Outcome: Efficient processes and effective task management, though sometimes lacking the visionary perspective needed for long-term success.

Developing Leadership Skills

Self-Reflection: Anumita frequently reflects on her strengths and weaknesses, pinpointing areas for improvement in her leadership approach.

Outcome: Enhanced self-awareness and ongoing personal growth.

Solicit Feedback: Anumita encourages feedback from her team, mentors, and peers. She utilizes constructive criticism to enhance her leadership abilities.

Outcome: Improved leadership effectiveness and stronger relationships with team members.

Continuous Learning: Anumita engages in leadership workshops and training programs to explore various leadership theories and practices.

Outcome: Expanded knowledge and skills, enabling her to adapt to diverse leadership challenges.

Cultivate Empathy: Anumita strives to understand and empathize with her team members, nurturing a supportive environment.

Outcome: Stronger relationships and increased team cohesion.

Develop Relationships: Anumita invests time in cultivating and nurturing strong relationships with her team members, building trust and respect.

Outcome: Improved team dynamics and a positive organizational culture.

Embrace Challenges: Anumita embraces new projects and roles within the organization, seizing opportunities to lead in varied settings.

Outcome: Personal growth and acquisition of new leadership skills.

Mentorship: Anumita engages a mentor who offers guidance and support as she refines her leadership abilities.

Outcome: Valuable insights and perspectives contributing to her leadership development.

By implementing diverse leadership styles, understanding power dynamics, and distinguishing between leadership and management, Anumita adeptly navigates the challenges at Do Good Foundation. Through continual development of her leadership skills and adaptation of her approach to suit her team's requirements, she emerges as a more influential and accomplished leader and manager.

CONCLUSION

Comprehending leadership styles, power dynamics, the disparity between leadership and management, and strategies for enhancing leadership skills is paramount for those aspiring to lead effectively. Leadership involves inspiring and motivating individuals, while management concentrates on organizing and coordinating resources. Both components are pivotal for organizational achievement. By continually refining your leadership skills and tailoring your approach to suit your team's needs, you can emerge as a more influential and accomplished leader.

------------- Multiple Choice Type Questions --------------

Q1. Which leadership style involves engaging team members in the decision-making process?

   A. Authoritative Leadership
   B. Participative Leadership
   C. Transformational Leadership
   D. Transactional Leadership

Q2. What type of power stems from an individual's role or title within an organization?

   A. Expert Power
   B. Referent Power
   C. Positional Power
   D. Coercive Power

Q3. Which leadership style focuses on routine tasks and utilizes rewards and penalties to manage performance?

   A. Authoritative Leadership
   B. Participative Leadership
   C. Transformational Leadership
   D. Transactional Leadership

Q4. Which of the following is NOT a characteristic of transformational leadership?

    A. Articulating a compelling vision

    B. Leading by example

    C. Utilizing rewards and penalties

    D. Encouraging innovation

Q5. In the context of leadership vs. management, which of the following best describes management?

    A. Envisioning, motivating, and inspiring individuals

    B. Planning, organizing, and coordinating resources

    C. Focusing on long-term goals and the big picture

    D. Cultivating relationships and promoting innovation

Q6. Which strategy is NOT mentioned as a way to develop leadership skills?

    A. Self-Reflection

    B. Soliciting Feedback

    C. Reducing team size

    D. Continuous Learning

Q7. What type of power involves the capacity to enforce consequences or punishments?

    A. Expert Power

    B. Referent Power

    C. Coercive Power

    D. Reward Power

Q8. Servant leadership primarily focuses on:

   A. Making decisions independently and expecting compliance

   B. Prioritizing the needs of team members and concentrating on serving others

   C. Engaging team members in the decision-making process

   D. Leading by example and articulating a compelling vision

-------------------- Match The Following --------------------

Q1. Match the following types of power with their descriptions:

1. Positional Power	A. Power based on the ability to dispense rewards.
2. Expert Power	B. Power derived from an individual's skills, knowledge, and expertise.
3. Referent Power	C. Power originating from personal traits and relationships.
4. Coercive Power	D. Power stemming from an individual's role or title within an organization.
5. Reward Power	E. Power involving the capacity to enforce consequences or punishments.

Q2. Match the following leadership styles with their characteristics:

1. Authoritative Leadership	A. Engage team members in the decision-making process.
2. Participative Leadership	B. Inspire and motivate teams by articulating a compelling vision.
3. Transformational Leadership	C. Make decisions independently and expect compliance.
4. Transactional Leadership	D. Concentrate on routine tasks and utilize rewards and penalties.
5. Servant Leadership	E. Prioritize the needs of team members and concentrate on serving others.

CHAPTER 17

THEORY X AND THEORY Y

INTRODUCTION

Within the field of management theory, Douglas McGregor's seminal work, The Human Side of Enterprise (1960), provides significant insights into human motivation and behaviour at work through his Theory X and Theory Y frameworks. These theories present contrasting perspectives that profoundly influence management practices and organizational cultures.

Make sure to answer all the questions given at the end of the chapter. This will help you evaluate your understanding of the topic and decide whether you need a quick review or a more detailed study.

THEORY X: THE PESSIMISTIC OUTLOOK

Theory X contains a cynical viewpoint of human nature, portraying employees as inherently lazy, lacking ambition, averse to responsibility, and in need of constant supervision. This theory posits that external rewards, such as money and fear of punishment, are the primary motivators for employees. The core tenets of Theory X include:

Disdain for Work: Employees inherently dislike work and will evade it whenever possible.

Lack of Drive: Workers prefer to be directed, shun responsibilities, and exhibit minimal ambition.

Dependency on Oversight: Employees necessitate close supervision and stringent control mechanisms.

External Motivation: Employees are primarily driven by external incentives like pay, job security, and the threat of punishment.

Exemplifying Theory X in Action

In an environment compliant with Theory X principles, such as a factory setting, stringent monitoring through surveillance and frequent checks is common. There are rigid rules, strict schedules, and minimal autonomy for workers. Performance is measured against stringent targets, with non-compliance promptly met with disciplinary measures.

Illustrative Scenario: Traditional Manufacturing Plant

At a conventional manufacturing facility, a hierarchical management structure is in place where workers are assigned repetitive tasks with detailed instructions to be strictly followed. The key performance metric is productivity, and any deviation from preset standards results in penalties or reprimands. For instance, in automotive assembly lines, strict production quotas must be adhered to, with performance under constant scrutiny. Deviations from these quotas can lead to warnings, reduced bonuses, or even termination.

THEORY Y: THE OPTIMISTIC PERSPECTIVE

In contrast to Theory X, Theory Y presents an optimistic outlook on employees, viewing them as naturally motivated individuals who enjoy their work, possess creativity, and can be self-directed. Theory Y asserts that employees can be entrusted with responsibilities and are driven by internal factors. The core principles of Theory Y include:

Inherent Work Ethic: For most individuals, work is as natural as recreation or leisure.

Self-Guidance: People exhibit self-control and self-direction when committed to objectives.

Commitment: Dedication to goals is influenced by the rewards associated with their accomplishment.

Creativity and Innovation: The average individual is inherently creative and resourceful, capable of solving organizational challenges.

Demonstration of Theory Y in Practice

Consider a technology start up embodying Theory Y principles, where employees are granted substantial autonomy to select projects and work schedules. The management cultivates a collaborative atmosphere that encourages free idea exchange and prizes innovation. Performance is assessed based on outcomes rather than processes, motivating employees to take initiative and explore new ideas.

Illustrative Scenario: Google

At Google, the "20% time" policy empowered engineers to allocate a fifth of their work time to projects of personal interest. This policy led to the development of successful products like Gmail and Google News. By entrusting employees to pursue meaningful and innovative projects, Google exemplifies Theory Y principles. The autonomy granted to employees resulted in heightened job satisfaction and substantial innovations, underscoring the positive impact of trusting and empowering employees on organizational success.

Comparison and Ramifications

Management Approach

Theory X: This perspective often leads to an authoritarian management style, emphasizing control and command as primary tools. Managers under Theory X typically engage in micro-management to ensure adherence to rules.

Theory Y: Advocates of Theory Y tend to adopt a participative management style that encourages employee involvement in decision-making. These managers act as facilitators, promoting trust and collaboration within the workplace.

Organizational Atmosphere

Theory X: Organizations embodying Theory X principles may exhibit a hierarchical structure, characterized by strict rules, low morale, high turnover rates, and an emphasis on procedures.

Theory Y: Companies following Theory Y tend to have a flatter organizational structure, promoting an inclusive culture that boosts job satisfaction, promotes creativity, and reduces turnover rates.

CASE STUDY: APPLICATION OF THEORY X AND THEORY Y AT ALPHATECH

Context

Alpha-Tech, a medium-sized technology firm, grappled with reduced workforce morale and efficiency. To address this, the company leadership opted to test Douglas McGregor's Theory X and Theory Y methodologies within two separate departments to evaluate their influence on performance and employee contentment.

Theory X in the Customer Support Department

In the Customer Support Department, the implementation of Theory X led to the establishment of a closely monitored working environment. Employees were continuously observed, with their performance metrics meticulously monitored. Strict protocols and inflexible guidelines were enforced, and any deviations from standards were met with immediate disciplinary measures. External incentives, like bonuses for meeting targets, and threats of repercussions for subpar performance, were used to motivate employees.

Theory Y in the Research and Development (R&D) Department

On the other hand, the Research and Development (R&D) Department embraced Theory Y principles, granting employees significant autonomy. Team members were encouraged to define their objectives, select projects aligned with their interests, and engage in open collaboration. Management prioritized outcomes over processes, nurturing an environment of trust and ingenuity. Employees were motivated by intrinsic rewards, such as meaningful project assignments and the freedom to experiment with new concepts.

Outcomes

The implementation of Theory X in the customer support department initially resulted in increased productivity but had a notable negative impact on employee morale. Reports of high stress levels and dissatisfaction surfaced, leading to a surge in employee turnover. Workers felt unappreciated and excessively monitored, which led to reduced engagement and creativity in problem-solving.

Conversely, the R&D department experienced heightened innovation and job satisfaction through the Theory Y approach. This methodology led to the successful completion of multiple projects, with employees feeling empowered and inspired. The inclusive atmosphere promoted creativity, cooperation, and a strong dedication to organizational objectives. Turnover rates remained low, and employees expressed considerable job satisfaction.

The experiment at AlphaTech underscored the drawbacks of a Theory X approach in sustaining long-term employee contentment and retention, despite short-term productivity gains. Meanwhile, the Theory Y approach illustrated the advantages of empowering employees, cultivating a positive corporate culture, and driving innovation. This case emphasizes the necessity of aligning management practices with job characteristics and employee needs to achieve enduring success.

CONCLUSION

Theory X and Theory Y present divergent approaches to managing human behavior in the workplace. While Theory X underscores control, supervision, and external motivation, effective for environments requiring strict adherence, it often yields low morale and high turnover. Conversely, Theory Y asserts that trust, autonomy, and avenues for personal growth drive motivation and creativity, promoting collaborative and innovative organizational cultures with enhanced job satisfaction and retention. Modern management trends increasingly favor Theory Y, acknowledging that empowering employees enhances long-term success. Balancing both theories enables managers to tailor strategies to fit their workforce's needs, enhancing productivity and achieving organizational objectives.

-------------- **Multiple Choice Type Questions** --------------

Q1. Which of the following best describes Theory X in management?

A. Employees are naturally motivated and enjoy their work.
B. Employees are seen as lazy and in need of constant supervision.
C. Management encourages autonomy and trust within the workplace.
D. Companies promote an inclusive culture and boost job satisfaction.

Q2. What is the primary motivator for employees according to Theory X?

A. Internal factors such as personal growth
B. External rewards like money and fear of punishment
C. Collaborative atmosphere and free idea exchange
D. Dedication to organizational goals

Q3. Which management style is associated with Theory X?

A. Participative management
B. Authoritarian management
C. Facilitative management
D. Collaborative management

Q4. What organizational structure characterizes companies following Theory Y?

A. Hierarchical structure with strict rules
B. Flatter organizational structure promoting inclusivity
C. Rigorous surveillance and frequent checks
D. Strict schedules and minimal autonomy for workers

Q5. Which theory emphasizes trust, autonomy, and personal growth?

A. Theory X
B. Theory Y
C. Both Theory X and Theory Y
D. Neither Theory X nor Theory Y

Q6. What approach does Theory Y advocate in managing human behaviour?

A. Control and supervision
B. Micro-management
C. Authoritarian style
D. Participative management

Q7. What type of atmosphere does Theory X typically create within an organization?

A. Inclusive culture with high job satisfaction
B. Low morale and high turnover rates
C. Collaborative atmosphere promoting innovation
D. Reduced turnover rates and increased creativity

Q8. Which theory emphasizes adherence to strict rules and procedures?

A. Theory X
B. Theory Y
C. Both Theory X and Theory Y
E. Neither Theory X nor Theory Y

-------------------- **Match The Following** --------------------

Q1. Match the management approach with its associated theory:

1. Theory X	A. Participative management style
2. Theory Y	B. Authoritarian management style

CHAPTER 18

POLARITY MANAGEMENT

INTRODUCTION

In the realm of leadership and organizational development, the practice of managing polarities offers a nuanced approach to navigating complex, paradoxical challenges. Unlike problems that can be definitively solved, polarities are interdependent pairs of values or perspectives that require ongoing management. They represent chronic issues that cannot be resolved by favouring one pole over the other but necessitate a dynamic balance to harness the benefits of both poles.

Make sure to answer all the questions given at the end of the chapter. This will help you evaluate your understanding of the topic and decide whether you need a quick review or a more detailed study.

UNDERSTANDING POLARITIES

Polarities, also termed dilemmas or paradoxes, depict competing yet interdependent values. Examples include stability versus change, autonomy versus control, and global standardization versus local adaptation. Each pole in a polarity has its own positive and negative aspects. Effective polarity management entails leveraging the strengths of both poles while mitigating their drawbacks.

For instance, in the polarity of stability versus change, stability offers consistency and reliability but can lead to rigidity and stagnation if overly emphasized. On the other hand, change leads to innovation and adaptability but can result in chaos and burnout if not balanced with stability. The goal is not to select one pole over the other but to find a way to derive benefits from both.

THE POLARITY MAP

A vital tool in polarity management is the Polarity Map, devised by Barry Johnson. This map aids in visualizing the dynamic interplay between the two poles and typically comprises four quadrants.

Upper Left Quadrant (Positive aspects of Pole 1): Highlighting the benefits and desired outcomes of prioritizing one pole. For example, in stability, these could include consistency, reliability, and predictability.

Upper Right Quadrant (Positive aspects of Pole 2): Focusing on the benefits and desired outcomes of the opposite pole. In the case of change, these might bound innovation, flexibility, and growth.

Lower Left Quadrant (Negative aspects of Pole 1): Listing the potential downsides or risks of overemphasizing Pole 1. Over prioritizing stability can lead to rigidity, resistance to change, and stagnation.

Lower Right Quadrant (Negative aspects of Pole 2): Outlining the downsides or risks of overemphasizing Pole 2. For change, these could involve chaos, lack of direction, and burnout.

By mapping out these quadrants, leaders can enhance their understanding of the dynamics at play and make more informed decisions that strike a balance between the benefits and risks of each pole.

STRATEGIES FOR MANAGING POLARITIES

Recognize and Name the Polarity: The initial step in managing a polarity is acknowledging its existence. Leaders must identify the competing values and recognize that neither can be eliminated.

Understand the Benefits and Risks: Utilize the Polarity Map to articulate the positive and negative aspects of each pole. This aids in comprehending the full spectrum of the polarity.

Engage Stakeholders: Involve various stakeholders in the discussion to acquire diverse perspectives. This collective understanding inculcates a more holistic approach to managing the polarity.

Monitor Indicators: Identify indicators that signal when the balance is tilting too far towards one pole. This aids in making timely adjustments before the downsides become detrimental.

Create Action Plans: Formulate strategies and action plans to maintain the balance. This includes setting up systems, processes, and behaviours that encourage movement between the poles as needed.

Embrace Continuous Learning: Polarity management is an ongoing process. Leaders must remain vigilant and adaptable, continuously learning and adjusting as circumstances evolve.

ROLE OF LEADERSHIP IN POLARITY MANAGEMENT

Effective polarity management demands a specific leadership mind-set. Leaders must embrace complexity and ambiguity, recognizing that some challenges cannot be solved with a linear approach. They need to develop a culture that values both/and thinking over either/or thinking, encouraging collaboration and open dialogue.

Leadership in polarity management also requires humility and a willingness to continually learn and adapt. Leaders must acknowledge that no single approach is perfect and that success lies in the ability to navigate the tension between competing values.

CASE STUDY 1: UNDERSTANDING POLARITIES THROUGH BREATHING

Breathing is a fundamental physiological process that illustrates the concept of polarities exceptionally well. Breathing involves two primary actions: inhaling and exhaling. These actions are interdependent, complementary, and necessary for sustaining life.

Key Characteristics of Breathing as a Polarity

Interdependence: Inhaling and exhaling are actions that rely on each other. You cannot just inhale without exhaling, and vice versa. They form an interdependent system.

Complementarity: While inhaling and exhaling are opposites, they complement each other. Inhaling brings oxygen into the lungs, which is essential for cellular respiration, while exhaling expels carbon dioxide, a waste product of this process.

Dynamic Balance: Effective breathing involves a continuous, dynamic balance between inhaling and exhaling. This balance is not static but adapts to the body's needs, such as during rest, exercise, or stress.

Inhaling Purpose: To bring oxygen into the body

Process:

Diaphragm contracts and moves downward.

Ribcage expands.

Air pressure in the lungs decreases, allowing air to flow in.

Positive Aspects: Oxygenates the blood, providing energy for cellular processes. Supports cognitive and physical functions.

Negative Aspects (if only inhaling): Buildup of carbon dioxide in the body. Potential for hyperventilation and dizziness.

Exhaling Purpose: To expel carbon dioxide from the body

Process:

Diaphragm relaxes and moves upward.

Ribcage contracts.

Air pressure in the lungs increases, pushing air out.

Positive Aspects:

Removes carbon dioxide, a metabolic waste product. Helps maintain pH balance in the blood.

Negative Aspects (if only exhaling):

Depletion of oxygen in the body.

Potential for suffocation and loss of consciousness.

The body naturally manages the polarity of breathing through the respiratory system, which maintains a balance between inhaling and exhaling. The metaphor of breathing illustrates the concept of polarities as described by Barry Johnson in "Polarity Management." Just as inhaling and exhaling are interdependent actions that sustain life, other polarities in personal and organizational contexts require a similar balanced approach. Recognizing, mapping, and managing these polarities can lead to more effective and resilient systems, whether in breathing or in broader applications.

CASE STUDY 2:

EXPLORING THE BALANCE BETWEEN TEAM UNITY AND PERSONAL FREEDOM AT CREATIVE SOLUTIONS LTD.

Context

Creative Solutions Ltd., a medium-sized advertising agency, is renowned for its inventive campaigns and collaborative ethos. Nonetheless, the organization grappled with a persistent dilemma: harmonizing collective team aspirations with the distinct needs of its members. While the solidarity of the team is fundamental for synchronized endeavours and dependable outcomes, the independence of individuals is vital for nurturing ingenuity and individual progression.

Recognizing the Contradiction

Under the guidance of CEO Aastik, the leadership team acknowledged the dichotomy between the team's necessities (unity, cooperation, synergy) and the desires of individual team members (freedom, creativity, self-expression). They recognized that prioritizing team unity excessively could stifle personal innovation, whereas an excessive focus on individual autonomy might compromise team cohesion and harmony.

Utilizing the Contradiction Map

Aastik introduced the Contradiction Map to visually map out the interactive relationship between team unity and individual freedom. The team delineated the following four quadrants:

Upper Left Quadrant (Positive facets of Team Unity): Synchronized efforts, dependable outcomes, robust collaboration, and shared objectives.

Upper Right Quadrant (Positive facets of Individual Freedom): Ingenuity, personal development, innovation, and job fulfilment.

Lower Left Quadrant (Negative facets of Team Unity): Hindered creativity, group mentality, uniformity, and lack of personal expression.

Lower Right Quadrant (Negative facets of Individual Freedom): Disarray, lack of cohesion, conflicting priorities, and diminished collaboration.

Engaging Stakeholders

Aastik and his team engaged diverse stakeholders, including team leads, creative directors, and individual contributors, to garner a spectrum of viewpoints. Through workshops and feedback sessions, they pinpointed areas where the equilibrium between team unity and individual freedom was either robust or needed fine-tuning.

Monitoring Metrics

The leadership team established key metrics to assess the equilibrium, encouraging team project success rates, individual appraisals, staff engagement surveys, and feedback concerning joint efforts. By monitoring these metrics vigilantly, they could detect imbalances and promptly make adjustments.

Developing Action Plans

To sustain the equilibrium, the team formulated targeted strategies. For team unity, they concentrated on enhancing collaborative platforms, organizing routine team-building events, and setting clear common objectives. Regarding individual freedom, they encouraged personal project time, provided flexible work setups, and nurtured a culture that appreciated and acknowledged individual contributions.

Embracing Continuous Learning

Aastik underscored the significance of continual learning and adaptability. The leadership team committed to regular evaluations of the polarity management strategy, being open to feedback and willing to adapt their approach as required. They nurtured a culture that prized both/and thinking, urging employees to embrace the intricacies of balancing team and individual needs.

Outcome

Through adept management of the contradiction between team unity and individual freedom, Creative Solutions Ltd. witnessed substantial enhancements in both team productivity and individual contentment. The organization upheld a sturdy, cohesive team milieu while concurrently encouraging individual ingenuity and advancement. Employee engagement and contentment soared as team members felt nurtured in an integrated environment that also valued their individual contributions.

Creative Solutions Ltd. showcased the efficacy of polarity management in navigating the intricate endeavour of harmonizing team unity with individual freedom. By acknowledging and addressing this contradiction, the company heightened its resilience, adaptability, and overall triumph. This case study underscores the significance of polarity management in ensuring a lively and innovative workplace where both team and individual requisites are aptly balanced.

CONCLUSION

Polarity management is a crucial skill for contemporary leaders grappling with a world of increasing complexity and interdependence. By comprehending and leveraging the dynamic interplay between polarities, leaders can establish more resilient and adaptive organizations. The capacity to balance competing values is not merely a strategic advantage but a necessity for sustainable success.

In summary, polarity management involves recognizing the inherent tensions within organizational life and learning to navigate them effectively. It necessitates a shift from problem-solving to managing ongoing dilemmas, assisting a mind-set of balance, adaptability, and continuous learning. Through tools such as the Polarity Map and strategies for dynamic balancing, leaders can harness the strengths of both poles and mitigate their downsides, propelling their organizations towards greater agility and resilience.

-------------- Multiple Choice Type Questions --------------

Q1. What is the primary goal of managing polarities in an organization?

A. To completely eliminate one pole
B. To find a dynamic balance between both poles
C. To favor one pole over the other
D. To avoid change entirely

Q2. In the context of polarity management, what does the term "polarity" refer to?

A. A temporary problem that can be easily solved
B. Interdependent pairs of values or perspectives requiring ongoing management
C. A situation where only one solution is correct
D. A straightforward challenge with a clear solution

Q3. Which of the following is NOT a part of the Polarity Map?

A. Upper Left Quadrant
B. Upper Right Quadrant
C. Middle Quadrant
D. Lower Right Quadrant

Q4. Why is it important for leaders to engage stakeholders in the polarity management process?

A. To delegate all decision-making to them
B. To acquire diverse perspectives and foster a holistic approach
C. To avoid making any decisions themselves
D. To minimize the complexity of the situation

Q5. Which strategy involves identifying indicators that signal when the balance is tilting too far towards one pole?

A. Recognize and Name the Polarity
B. Monitor Indicators
C. Create Action Plans
D. Embrace Continuous Learning

Q6. What mind-set is required for effective polarity management in leadership?

A. Linear and problem-solving oriented
B. Either/or thinking
C. Both/and thinking
D. Avoidance of ambiguity and complexity

-------------------- **Match The Following** --------------------

Q1. Match the elements of the Polarity Map with their corresponding descriptions:

1. Outlining the downsides or risks of overemphasizing Pole 2.	A. Upper Left Quadrant
2. Listing the potential downsides or risks of overemphasizing Pole 1.	B. Upper Right Quadrant
3. Focusing on the benefits and desired outcomes of the opposite pole.	C. Lower Left Quadrant
4. Highlighting the benefits and desired outcomes of prioritizing one	D. Lower Right Quadrant pole.

CHAPTER 19

DECISION MAKING AND PROBLEM SOLVING

INTRODUCTION

Effective decision making and problem-solving are crucial abilities for addressing personal and professional challenges. This chapter examines different decision-making strategies and methods, highlights distinctions between individual and group decision-making, delves into problem-solving approaches, and discusses typical biases and mistakes encountered during decision-making processes.

Please make sure you make an effort to answer all the questions given in the chapter. This approach will help you evaluate your understanding of the topic and decide if a quick review or a more detailed study is required.

DECISION-MAKING MODELS AND TECHNIQUES

Decision-making models and techniques offer structures to make well-informed and organized decisions. Here are some common models:

Rational Decision Making Model

This model consists of a structured, methodical method for making decisions. It comprises:

Identifying the problem: Clearly outline the problem that requires attention.

Gathering information: Gather pertinent data and information.

Evaluating alternatives: Contemplate all potential solutions and their probable results.

Choosing the best alternative: Select the best solution to the issue.

Implementing the decision: Implement the selected solution.

Reviewing the decision: Assess the efficiency of the choice and make revisions as needed.

Intuitive Decision-Making Model

This model depends on intuition and instincts instead of structured analysis. It is commonly utilized for making rapid decisions when there is insufficient time for thorough analysis.

Decision Matrix

A decision matrix assists in comparing various options by evaluating them based on a predefined set of criteria. Each option is assigned a rating, and the total scores are calculated to identify the optimal choice.

Cost Benefit Analysis

This method requires evaluating the costs and benefits of each choice. The choice that yields the greatest net benefit is usually selected.

SWOT Analysis

This entails assessing the Strengths, Weaknesses, Opportunities, and Threats associated with a decision. It aids in comprehending the internal and external factors influencing the decision.

INDIVIDUAL VS. GROUP DECISION MAKING

Analysing the Strengths, Weaknesses, Opportunities, and Threats associated with a decision is crucial for comprehending the internal and external factors influencing the decision-making process.

Individual Decision Making

Advantages

Quicker decision making due to not needing consensus.

Defined accountability with a single individual responsible for decisions.

Simplified processes, resulting in fewer conflicts and distractions.

Disadvantages

Can be limited in perspective since it depends on the knowledge and experience of a single individual.

Prone to biases and blind spots.

Might miss out on alternative solutions because of a lack of diverse input.

Group Decision Making

Advantages

Facilitates a range of viewpoints and skills, contributing to more comprehensive decisions.

Encourage creativity and idea generation, potentially revealing inventive solutions.

Promotes collective accountability and endorsement, resulting in improved execution and backing.

Disadvantages

Decelerated process because of the requirement for discussion and agreement.

Hazard of groupthink, in which the quest for harmony results in subpar decisions.

Possibility of conflicts and differences of opinion, which may convolute the decision-making process.

PROBLEM-SOLVING PROCESSES

Problem-solving includes recognizing problems and discovering efficient solutions. These are the essential steps in the problem-solving procedure.

Identify the Problem

Define the problem clearly. Identifying the root cause is essential for discovering the appropriate solution.

Gather Information

Gather pertinent data and information regarding the issue. This involves grasping the context and any limitations.

Generate Solutions

Brainstorm potential solutions. Promote creativity and explore all possible options without making judgments at first.

Evaluate Solutions

Evaluate every solution considering factors like viability, expenses, timeframe, and prospective effects. Utilize instruments such as decision matrices or cost-benefit analysis to assess different choices.

Choose the Best Solution

Choose the solution that most effectively resolves the issue and aligns with the evaluation criteria.

Implement the Solution

Implement the selected solution. Create a plan and assign resources as required.

Review and Adjust

Monitor the execution and assess the outcomes. Modify as needed to ensure successful resolution of the issue.

BIASES AND ERRORS IN DECISION MAKING

Even when using structured methods, decision-making can still be impacted by different biases and mistakes. Understanding these factors can assist in reducing their effects.

Confirmation Bias

To avoid this bias, strive to embrace a variety of viewpoints and question your assumptions.

Anchoring Bias

When making decisions, it is important to not rely excessively on the initial piece of information you come across (referred to as the "anchor"). To prevent this, it is recommended to utilize information from various sources and refrain from forming quick judgments.

Overconfidence Bias

Overestimating one's knowledge or ability to predict outcomes can be minimized by seeking feedback and considering potential risks and uncertainties.

Availability Heuristic

Make decisions based on easily accessible information instead of actively looking for more pertinent data. To prevent this, carry out comprehensive research and take into account all relevant information.

Groupthink

The inclination towards harmony and uniformity in a group that can result in illogical choices. Encourage open discussions, differing viewpoints, and analytical thinking within the group.

Status Quo Bias

Preferring the status quo and being hesitant to adapt. To address this, consider the advantages of change and welcome fresh perspectives.

CASE STUDY: BOOSTING DECISION-MAKING AND PROBLEM-SOLVING CAPABILITIES AT XYZ LTD.

Context

XYZ Ltd., a medium-sized manufacturing enterprise, grappled with notable operational inefficiencies and diminished employee morale. To combat these challenges, the management team opted to refine their decision-making and problem-solving methods through the adoption of structured models and techniques. This approach targeted both individual and group decision-making behaviors while addressing prevalent biases.

Execution

The endeavour kicked off with instructional workshops introducing various decision-making models and techniques, such as the Rational Decision-Making Model, Decision Matrix, and SWOT Analysis. Employees received guidance on problem identification, data collection, solution generation and assessment, and the execution of optimal alternatives.

Individual Decision-Making

In situations necessitating swift resolutions, managers employed the Rational Decision-Making Model

Defining the Issue: Managers meticulously outlined concerns like delays in production.

Information Gathering: They amassed data related to production schedules, equipment performance, and workforce efficacy.

Assessing Options: Various alternatives, like equipment enhancements and staff training initiatives, were evaluated.

Selecting the Ideal Solution: The decision to upgrade machinery was finalized.

Implementation: Advanced equipment was procured and installed.

Evaluation: The machinery's impact on production efficiency was closely monitored.

Group Decision-Making

When confronted with intricate challenges, such as market expansion, a collaborative decision-making strategy was applied:

Idea Generation: A team was assembled to brainstorm potential markets.

Evaluation Process: A Decision Matrix facilitated comparisons based on factors like market size, competition, and profitability.

Optimal Choice: The team endorsed the market with the highest ranking.

Execution: A market penetration strategy was devised and put into action.

Review and Adjustment: Market performance was regularly assessed, with modifications implemented as necessary.

Bias Alleviation

The training program also emphasized the identification and mitigation of biases like confirmation bias, anchoring bias, and groupthink:

Confirmation Bias: Managers were urged to seek diverse viewpoints and challenge assumptions effectively.

Anchoring Bias: Decisions relied on information from diverse sources rather than initial data alone.

Groupthink: Encouragement of open dialogues and critical thinking ensured consideration of varied perspectives.

Results

The structured approach to decision-making and problem-solving yielded remarkable enhancements at XYZ Ltd. Production efficiency surged by 20%, employee morale saw an upturn owing to more inclusive decision-making practices, and the company's successful venture into a new market bolstered revenue by 15%. This case study underscores the effectiveness of structured models, group collaboration, and bias mitigation in fortifying decision-making and problem-solving competencies.

CONCLUSION

Effective decision making and problem solving skills are crucial in personal and professional settings alike. Understanding various decision making models and techniques is key to organizing the process and enhancing outcomes. Distinguishing between individual and group decision making enables the selection of the most suitable approach. Adhering to a structured problem solving process ensures thorough resolution of issues. Moreover, acknowledging common biases and errors in decision making can aid in reducing their influence and promoting more informed and reasoned decisions.

By refining these abilities, one can tackle challenges more successfully and attain superior results.

-------------- Multiple Choice Type Questions --------------

Q1. Which model involves a structured, methodical method for making decisions including steps like identifying the problem and gathering information?

    A. Intuitive Decision Making Model
    B. Rational Decision Making Model
    C. Cost-Benefit Analysis
    D. SWOT Analysis

Q2. What is the primary advantage of individual decision-making?

    A. Promotes creativity and idea generation
    B. Quicker decision making due to not needing consensus
    C. Facilitates a range of viewpoints and skills
    D. Fosters collective accountability and endorsement

Q3. Which bias involves overestimating one's own knowledge or ability to predict outcomes?

    A. Confirmation Bias
    B. Anchoring Bias
    C. Overconfidence Bias
    D. Availability Heuristic

Q4. What does the SWOT Analysis help with?

    A. Comparing various options by evaluating them based on a predefined set of criteria
    B. Evaluating the costs and benefits of each choice
    C. Assessing the strengths, weaknesses, opportunities, and threats associated with a decision
    D. Relying on intuition and instincts for making decisions

Q5. Which problem-solving step involves generating potential solutions and developing creativity?

    A. Identify the Problem
    B. Gather Information
    C. Generate Solutions
    D. Implement the Solution

Q6. What is a disadvantage of group decision making?

    A. Faster decision-making process
    B. Defined accountability
    C. Simplified processes
    D. Risk of groupthink

Q7. Which technique assists in comparing various options by evaluating them based on a predefined set of criteria?

    A. SWOT Analysis
    B. Decision Matrix
    C. Cost Benefit Analysis
    D. Intuitive Decision-Making Model

Q8. Which bias involves making decisions based on easily accessible information instead of seeking more relevant data?

    A. Confirmation Bias
    B. Anchoring Bias
    C. Availability Heuristic
    D. Status Quo Bias

-------------------- Match The Following --------------------

Q1. Match the following biases with their definitions:

1. Confirmation Bias	A. Relying too heavily on the first piece of information encountered.
2. Anchoring Bias	B. Overestimating one's own knowledge or ability to predict outcomes.
3. Overconfidence Bias	C. Preferring the current state of affairs and being resistant to change.
4. Availability Heuristic	D. Making decisions based on easily accessible information instead of seeking more relevant data.
5. Status Quo Bias	E. Seeking out information that confirms one's pre-existing beliefs.

Q2. Match the following decision-making models/techniques with their descriptions:

1. Rational Decision-Making Model	A. Assessing the strengths, weaknesses, opportunities, and threats associated with a decision.
2. Intuitive Decision-Making Model	B. Evaluating options based on a predefined set of criteria, assigning ratings, and calculating total scores.
3. Decision Matrix	C. Making decisions based on intuition and instincts rather than structured analysis.
4. Cost-Benefit Analysis	D. A structured, methodical approach involving steps like identifying the problem, gathering information, evaluating alternatives, and implementing the decision.
5. SWOT Analysis	E. Evaluating the costs and benefits of each option to select the one with the greatest net benefit.

CHAPTER 20

EFFECTIVENESS TO EXCELLENCE

INTRODUCTION

This chapter is drawn from Stephen R. Covey's renowned publication, "The 7 Habits of Highly Effective People," and wraps up with a concise summary of his subsequent work, "The 8th Habit." Covey's teachings on personal and professional growth offer a robust structure for attaining effectiveness and progressing towards excellence.

Ensure that you answer to all the questions presented in the chapter. This process will assist you in assessing your grasp of the subject matter and in determining whether a brief recap or a more thorough reading is necessary.

DESCRIPTION OF HABITS

Our character is shaped by our habits, which are enduring and often automatic behaviours that influence our effectiveness. Cultivating the seven habits of effectiveness guides us through various phases of character enhancement. Habits 1 to 3 represent the "private victory," as we evolve from dependence to independence by assuming accountability for our own lives. Habits 4 to 6 constitute the "public victory," where, after achieving independence, we learn to be interdependent and thrive alongside others. The seventh habit enables the rest by facilitating regular self-renewal.

PRIVATE VICTORY

The initial three habits center on self-discipline, accomplishing the personal triumphs necessary to progress from dependence to independence.

Habit 1: Be Proactive

"Be Proactive" is about having self-awareness and the ability to choose your response and response-ability. Focus on what you can control and take action.

Change begins internally, and effective individuals decide to enhance their lives by influencing what they can instead of merely reacting to external circumstances. This habit underscores the importance of taking the initiative and owning up to your actions.

Habit 2: Begin with the End in Mind

"Begin with the End in Mind" involves imagination and conscience. Start every process with a clear vision of your ultimate objective. Craft a personal mission statement based on principles and translate it into long-term goals aligned with those principles. This habit prompts individuals to define their life aspirations and progress towards them with a focused vision, ensuring their efforts resonate with their values and goals.

Habit 3: Put First Things First

"Put First Things First" requires willpower. Organize your life around your priorities. Allocate time to activities that support your personal mission, striking a balance between productivity and enhancing your capabilities. Identify your key life roles and allocate time for each of them. This habit emphasizes prioritizing tasks that contribute to your long-term objectives and values while sidestepping distractions and insignificant urgent matters.

PUBLIC VICTORY

Habits 4, 5, and 6 focus on interdependence and achieving public victories.

Habit 4: Think Win/Win

"Think Win/Win" contain an abundance mind-set. Stay true to your beliefs, values, and obligations while considering others' perspectives. Believe there is enough for everyone. Strive for agreements and relationships that are mutually advantageous. When a win/win agreement isn't feasible, recognize that choosing to walk away without a deal could be the best option. This habit plays a critical role in realising a work culture that champions win/win interactions among employees and discourages rewarding win/lose behaviour.

Habit 5: Seek First to Understand, Then to Be Understood

Seeking to understand first before seeking to be understood entails a balance of courage and consideration. Mastery of clear communication and active listening is crucial. Covey asserts that this habit is the cornerstone of effective interpersonal relationships. Effective listening involves empathetically comprehending both the emotions and intentions of others. The habit aims to shift focus from responding to truly understanding.

Habit 6: Synergize

"Synergize" contain the essence of creativity, creating outcomes greater than the sum of individual contributions. Through open and trustworthy communication, leverage diverse perspectives to produce collective excellence. Mutual trust and comprehension often resolve conflicts and yield superior solutions beyond individual capacity. This habit underscores the potency of collaboration and teamwork in achieving remarkable results.

Habit 7: Sharpen the Saw

"Sharpen the Saw" symbolizes the commitment to perpetual self-improvement and renewal to combat stagnation. Develop personal growth by nurturing a holistic lifestyle in physical, social/emotional, mental, and spiritual dimensions. Make time for personal development to enhance productivity and well-being. This habit underscores the significance of self-care and continuous growth for long-term effectiveness.

THE 8TH HABIT

Published in 2004 as a sequel to "The Seven Habits," Covey's book "The 8th Habit: From Effectiveness to Greatness" challenges the notion that effectiveness alone suffices in the "Knowledge Worker Age." It stresses the importance of individual fulfilment and leadership in inspiring others to find their purpose. The 8th habit invites individuals to unleash their potential and encourage others to do the same in a modern context.

CASE STUDY: ELEVATING ABC CORPORATION

Context

ABC Corporation, a mid-sized technology firm, encountered challenges related to employee engagement, productivity, and leadership development. In response, the executive team chose to incorporate Stephen R. Covey's teachings from "The 7 Habits of Highly Effective People" and "The 8th Habit" to boost individual and organizational efficiency.

Execution

Under the guidance of the Chief Human Resources Officer (CHRO), the HR department kick-started a holistic training program based on Covey's principles. This initiative was structured into two distinct phases: accomplishing private victory and public victory.

Private Victory

The initial phase concentrated on promoting self-discipline and self-sufficiency among the workforce.

Habit 1: Employees were motivated to assume responsibility for their duties and concentrate on aspects within their sphere of influence. Workshops on self-awareness and proactive conduct served to illustrate the significance of instigating positive transformations.

Habit 2: Employees formulated personal mission statements that resonated with the company's vision. This endeavor aided individuals in defining their long-term aspirations and aligning their daily endeavors accordingly.

Habit 3: Time management workshops underscored the importance of prioritizing tasks that contributed to personal and organizational aspirations. Employees acquired skills in balancing urgent tasks with important, enduring undertakings.

Public Victory

The subsequent phase stressed the values of collaboration and interconnectivity.

Habit 4: Training workshops were centered on developing a culture of shared advantage. Employees honed negotiation skills and tactics to craft win-win situations, promoting teamwork and collaboration.

Habit 5: Communication workshops placed emphasis on active listening and empathetic comprehension. Staff members practiced attentive listening to their peers' viewpoints before responding, thus nurturing better relationships and mitigating conflicts.

Habit 6: Team-building activities encouraged creativity and collaborative efforts. Employees were urged to leverage diverse viewpoints to tackle challenges and innovate, ultimately leading to heightened teamwork and productivity.

Habit 7: Routine self-renewal activities, like wellness initiatives and professional growth opportunities, were introduced. These schemes focused on holistic advancement, ensuring employees maintained physical, mental, and emotional well-being.

The 8th Habit

Embracing the principles of "The 8th Habit," the leadership team urged employees to discover their voices and inspire others. Leadership development programs aimed at assisting employees in identifying their purpose and serving as exemplary leaders.

Results: The incorporation of Covey's principles sparked a remarkable transformation at ABC Corporation. Employee engagement and productivity saw significant advancements, while leadership development endeavors promoted a culture of continuous progress and distinction. The emphasis on collaboration and interdependence led to ground-breaking solutions and collective triumph, establishing ABC Corporation as an industry frontrunner. This case study exemplifies the efficacy of Covey's doctrines in propelling personal and organizational evolution towards excellence.

CONCLUSION

Our habits shape our character, comprising knowledge, skills, and desire. Knowledge informs our actions, skills empower us to execute, and desire fuels our motivation. The Seven Habits guide us through stages of dependence, independence, and interdependence. While independence is often celebrated, interdependence is crucial in today's environment that necessitates teamwork and leadership. Mastering the Seven Habits not only enhances personal effectiveness but also contributes to collective success within organizations and communities.

------------ Multiple Choice Type Questions --------------

Q1. Which habit emphasizes taking the initiative and owning up to your actions?

- A. Begin with the End in Mind
- B. Be Proactive
- C. Put First Things First
- D. Sharpen the Saw

Q2. "Begin with the End in Mind" involves:

- A. Taking initiative and focusing on controllable factors
- B. Starting every endeavour with a clear vision of your ultimate objective
- C. Balancing productivity with capability enhancement
- D. Committing to perpetual self-improvement

Q3. Which habit is about organizing your life around your priorities and avoiding distractions?

- A. Think Win/Win
- B. Put First Things First
- C. Seek First to Understand, then to Be Understood
- D. Synergize

Q4. "Think Win/Win" promotes:

A. Mutual trust and comprehension
B. Creating outcomes greater than individual contributions
C. Agreements and relationships that are mutually advantageous
D. Regular self-renewal

Q5. Which habit emphasizes empathetic listening and understanding others before being understood?

A. Be Proactive
B. Begin with the End in Mind
C. Seek First to Understand, then to Be Understood
D. Synergize

Q6. "Synergize" involves:

A. Maintaining a balance of courage and consideration
B. Leveraging diverse perspectives through open communication
C. Taking action based on what can be controlled
D. Starting with a clear vision of ultimate objectives

Q7. What does "Sharpen the Saw" symbolize?

A. Creating mutually advantageous relationships
B. Organizing life around priorities
C. Committing to perpetual self-improvement and renewal
D. Starting with a clear vision of the end goal

Q8. According to Covey, what is the cornerstone of effective interpersonal relationships?

A. Thinking Win/Win
B. Putting First Things First
C. Seeking First to Understand, then to Be Understood
D. Synergizing

-------------------- Match The Following --------------------

Q1. Match the following habits with their descriptions:

1. Be Proactive	A. Organize your life around your priorities, balancing productivity and capability enhancement.
2. Begin with the End in Mind	B. Strive for mutually advantageous agreements and relationships.
3. Put First Things First	C. Leverage diverse perspectives to produce collective excellence through open communication.
4. Think Win/Win	D. Commit to perpetual self-improvement and renewal in all aspects of life.
5. Seek First to Understand, Then to Be Understood	E. Start with a clear vision of your ultimate objective, crafting a personal mission statement.
6. Synergize	F. Master clear communication and active listening to understand before seeking to be understood.
7. Sharpen the Saw	G. Focus on what you can control and take action, owning up to your actions.

CHAPTER 21

RETURN ON TRAINING INVESTMENT

INTRODUCTION

Return on Training Investment (ROTI) is gaining importance as organizations strive to rationalize and enhance their investments in employee training. This chapter explores ROTI from an employer's standpoint where evaluating training outcomes is more straightforward.

Make sure to make an effort to answer all the questions found in the chapter. This approach can help you evaluate your understanding of the material and decide if a quick review or a more detailed study is needed.

DEFINING ROTI

ROTI is typically examined using an accounting-based cost/benefit analysis. Training costs contain various expenses such as course development, instructional materials, salaries, travel, and productivity-related costs. Challenges to conducting ROTI analyses include the subjective nature of training benefits, the delayed realization of benefits, lack of expertise for analysis, and disruptions caused by data collection. However, conducting ROTI analyses is essential to justify HR budgets, enhance training relevance, improve data-driven decision-making, and optimize training effectiveness.

TRAINING COSTS AND RETURNS

The costs and returns associated with training are multifaceted, including tangible and intangible aspects. While direct training costs for businesses include design, salaries, facilities, and materials, benefits range from improved productivity and quality to reduced supervision needs and increased promotions. For individuals, tangible costs involve training and materials, while intangible costs include productivity loss and potential turnover risks. Benefits for individuals include enhanced skills, morale, cooperation, and job satisfaction. ROTI is explained with numerous examples and case studies for deeper understanding of the subject matter.

KIRKPATRICK EVALUATION MODEL

The Kirkpatrick Evaluation Model, developed by Donald Kirkpatrick, is a widely adopted framework for evaluating the effectiveness of training programs. The model assesses training across four levels: reactions, learning, behaviour, and results, with an optional fifth level focusing on Return on Investment (ROI). Let's delve into each level with an illustrative example.

Level 1: Reaction

This stage gauges participants' responses to the training session, focusing on their immediate reactions and satisfaction with the experience.

Example: Consider a scenario where a company offers a customer service training program for its staff. At the program's conclusion, participants are asked to fill out a survey. The survey might include questions like:

How satisfied were you with the training material?

Did the trainer effectively deliver the content?

Was the training environment conducive for learning?

If the majority of respondent's express high satisfaction and positive feedback, it suggests that the training was well-received.

Level 2: Learning

This level assesses the degree to which participants have grasped the desired knowledge, skills, and attitudes from the training. It involves evaluating the acquired learnings during the training.

Example: In the same customer service training program, participants undergo a pre-test before the session and a post-test afterward. These tests evaluate their understanding of customer service principles and practices. A significant improvement in post-test scores compared to pre-test scores indicates successful learning from the training.

Level 3: Behavior

This step evaluates the application of acquired knowledge by participants in their work environment. It looks at behavioral changes and the practical impact of the training on performance.

Example: Months after the customer service training, supervisors observe and assess employees' interactions with customers. They watch for behaviors taught in the training, such as active listening, empathy, and problem-solving abilities. Consistent enhancement in these behaviors signals that the training has positively influenced on-the-job performance.

Level 4: Results

This level gauges the training's impact on organizational outcomes. It examines the overall effectiveness of the training in achieving business objectives.

Example: The organization monitors key performance indicators (KPIs) related to customer service, such as customer satisfaction scores, complaint resolution times, and repeat customer rates. A notable improvement in these KPIs following the training indicates that the program has contributed to enhanced organizational outcomes.

Level 5: Return on Investment (ROI)

Though not originally part of Kirkpatrick's model, some organizations include a fifth level to measure the financial ROI of the training. This level compares the monetary returns of the training to its costs.

Example: The company calculates the expenses incurred for the customer service training, containing materials, trainer fees, and participants' time. Subsequently, they quantify the financial gains, like increased sales from repeat customers and savings from fewer customer complaints. By comparing these benefits to the costs, the organization determines the ROI of the training initiative.

CASE STUDY 1

Let's envision a retail company implementing a customer service training program to enhance employee skills and boost customer satisfaction. Here's how the Kirkpatrick Evaluation Model would come into play:

Reaction: Feedback surveys post-training reveal that 90% of participants found the training engaging and relevant.

Learning: Pre-test and post-test outcomes show a 40% increase in knowledge of effective customer service techniques.

Behavior: Supervisors note consistent application of training techniques by employees, such as welcoming customers warmly and resolving issues efficiently.

Results: Customer satisfaction ratings surge by 25%, and the number of repeat customers rises by 15% over six months.

ROI: The training program costs Rs10,000, while the financial benefits amount to Rs50,000 from increased sales and reduced complaint resolutions. Calculating the ROI ((Rs50,000 - Rs10,000) /Rs10,000) shows a 400% return.

By leveraging the Kirkpatrick Evaluation Model, the retail company can convincingly showcase the value of its training investment, demonstrating advancements at each level, from participant satisfaction to concrete business outcomes.

THE BELL SYSTEM APPROACH

The Bell System Approach, an expansion of Kirkpatrick's model, enhances the assessment of training effectiveness by concentrating on four primary areas: reaction, capability, application, and worth outcomes. This method provides a more holistic evaluation by not only measuring immediate feedback and learning but also scrutinizing how the training is utilized in the workplace and its overall value in relation to costs.

Level 1: Reaction

This stage evaluates participants' immediate responses to the training, akin to Kirkpatrick's model. It assesses their contentment with the training content, delivery, and setting.

Example: A telecommunications firm introduces a training scheme on advanced networking methods for its technical support employees. After the training concludes, participants respond to a survey that asks:

How satisfied are you with the entire training experience?

Was the trainer well-informed and engaging?

Did the training materials and activities meet your expectations?

Positive satisfaction scores from participants signify a favorable initial reaction to the training.

Level 2: Capability

This stage measures the degree to which participants have acquired the necessary knowledge and skills from the training. It focuses on their ability to complete tasks and grasp the concepts taught during the training.

Example: Participants in the networking training program undergo a skills assessment test before and after the training. The test evaluates their comprehension of advanced networking concepts, troubleshooting methods, and equipment configuration. A notable improvement in post-training test scores compared to pre-training scores indicates an enhancement in participants' capabilities.

Level 3: Application

This stage assesses how effectively participants implement their newly acquired skills and knowledge in their job responsibilities. It scrutinizes whether the training has resulted in observable changes in behavior and performance at work.

Example: Several months after the networking training, supervisors observe and evaluate the performance of the technical support staff. They look for specific behaviors such as enhanced problem-solving abilities, expedited resolution of network issues, and improved customer interactions. Consistent application of the learned skills in real-world scenarios indicates that the training has succeeded in altering job performance.

Level 4: Worth Outcomes

This stage evaluates the overall value of the training to the organization. It gauges the worth outcomes by assessing the impact of the training on business objectives and determining whether the benefits outweigh the costs.

Example: The telecommunications company monitors key performance indicators (KPIs) such as network uptime, customer satisfaction scores, and the number of support tickets resolved. If these KPIs demonstrate significant enhancement after the training, it implies that the training has positively affected the organization's performance. Moreover, the company calculates the return on investment (ROI) by contrasting the cost of the training program with the financial gains derived from improved performance and customer satisfaction.

CASE STUDY 2

A telecommunications company aims to enhance the technical skills of its support staff through an advanced networking training program. Here's how the Bell System Approach would be implemented:

Reaction: Participants submit a feedback survey post-training, with 85% expressing high satisfaction with the training content and delivery.

Capability: Pre-training and post-training assessments reveal a 50% enhancement in participants' knowledge and skills related to advanced networking techniques.

Application: Supervisors notice that technical support staff are effectively applying their new skills, resulting in a 30% decrease in network issue resolution time and enhanced customer service interactions.

Worth Outcomes: The company tracks performance metrics such as network uptime, customer satisfaction scores, and the number of resolved support tickets. Over six months, they observe a 20% rise in network uptime and a 15% increase in customer satisfaction. The training program costs Rs20,000, and the financial benefits, including enhanced efficiency and customer retention, amount to Rs80,000. The ROI is computed as (Rs80,000 - Rs20,000) / Rs20,000 = 300%.

By leveraging the Bell System Approach, the telecommunications company can evidently showcase the effectiveness and value of its training program, depicting advancements at each stage from participant contentment to tangible business outcomes and financial gains.

BALANCED SCORECARD

The Balanced Scorecard, established by Robert Kaplan and David Norton, serves as a strategic management tool aligning training outcomes with an organization's objectives through four key perspectives: financial, customer, internal processes, and learning and growth. This method enables organizations to ensure that training programs contribute effectively to reaching strategic goals and supports in-depth performance monitoring. Let's delve into each perspective with an illustrative example.

Financial Perspective

The financial aspect concentrates on how training impacts an organization's financial performance, measuring contributions to enhanced financial outcomes like increased revenue, cost reduction, and greater profitability.

Example: In an instance, a retail firm conducts sales training to drive revenue growth, with metrics including:

Rise in sales revenue

Cut in sales-related costs

Enhancement in profit margins

After the training, the company observes a 15% surge in sales revenue and a 10% cut in customer acquisition costs, resulting in improved profit margins.

Customer Perspective

This perspective evaluates how training influences customer satisfaction and loyalty, focusing on metrics like satisfaction scores, retention rates, and customer complaints.

Example: For the same retail company aiming to boost customer service, tracked metrics comprise:

Customer satisfaction scores

Customer retention rates

Number of customer complaints

Post-training, the company records a 20% upturn in satisfaction scores, a 15% increase in retention rates, and a 25% drop in customer complaints.

Internal Processes Perspective

The internal processes perspective examines how training bolsters the efficiency and effectiveness of internal operations by measuring enhancements in key business processes and operational efficiency.

Example: To optimize inventory management, the retail company provides specialized training to its inventory staff, tracking metrics such as:

Inventory turnover rate

Order fulfillment accuracy

Time required for restocking items

Following the training, the company witnesses a 30% improvement in inventory turnover rate, a 25% boost in order fulfillment accuracy, and a 20% reduction in restocking time.

Learning and Growth Perspective

Focusing on developing human capital, culture, and infrastructure, the learning and growth perspective measures advancements in employee skills, satisfaction, retention, and innovation capacity.

Example: The retail firm invests in continuous learning and development programs for employees, monitoring metrics like:

Employee skill levels

Employee satisfaction and engagement

Employee retention rates

Upon program implementation, the company notes a 40% spike in employee skill levels, a 30% rise in employee satisfaction and engagement, and a 20% drop in turnover rates.

CASE STUDY 3

Applying the Balanced Scorecard approach, a retail company aligns training programs with strategic objectives, targeting sales performance, customer service, inventory management, and employee development. Here's how each perspective is addressed:

Financial Perspective: After sales training, the company achieves a 15% increase in sales revenue and a 10% drop in customer acquisition costs, increasing profit margins.

Customer Perspective: Customer service training leads to a 20% spike in satisfaction scores, a 15% boost in retention rates, and a 25% decrease in complaints.

Internal Processes Perspective: Inventory management training brings about a 30% boost in inventory turnover rate, a 25% increase in order accuracy, and a 20% reduction in restocking time.

Learning and Growth Perspective: Learning programs lift employee skill levels by 40%, enhance satisfaction by 30%, and lower turnover by 20%.

Adopting the Balanced Scorecard ensures strategic alignment of training programs with organizational goals, supporting holistic performance monitoring to achieve long-term objectives across various domains ranging from financial performance and customer satisfaction to internal efficiency and employee development.

CONCLUSION

ROTI evaluation is crucial for assessing the impact and value of training investments. By considering both quantitative and qualitative gains using models like Kirkpatrick, the Bell System, and Balanced Scorecard, organizations can optimize their training initiatives and align employee development efforts with strategic objectives.

-------------- **Multiple Choice Type Questions** --------------

Q1. What is ROTI typically examined using?

A. Employee surveys
B. Cost/benefit analysis
C. Performance reviews
D. Market research

Q2. Which of the following is NOT a direct training cost for businesses?

A. Design
B. Salaries
C. Tuition fees
D. Facilities

Q3. What is a significant challenge in conducting ROTI analyses?

A. Overabundance of data
B. The subjective nature of training benefits
C. The simplicity of data collection
D. The immediate realization of benefits

Q4. Which ROTI model evaluates training at levels of reactions, learning, behaviour, and results, with an additional level for ROI?

A. The Bell System Approach
B. Balanced Scorecard
C. Kirkpatrick Evaluation Model
D. Cost/Benefit Analysis

Q5. What does the Bell System Approach assess in addition to reaction?

A. Motivation, learning, and growth
B. Financial, customer, and internal processes
C. Capability, application, and worth outcomes
D. Design, facilities, and materials

Q6. Which model was introduced by Robert Kaplan and David Norton?

A. Kirkpatrick Evaluation Model
B. Balanced Scorecard
C. The Bell System Approach
D. Cost/Benefit Analysis

Q7. Which of the following is an intangible benefit of training for individuals?

   A. Reduced supervision needs

   B. Tuition fees

   C. Increased promotions

   D. Job satisfaction

Q8. Why is ROTI evaluation crucial for organizations?

   A. It simplifies the training process

   B. It helps justify HR budgets and optimize training effectiveness

   C. It increases employee turnover

   D. It reduces the need for training altogether

-------------------- **Match The Following** --------------------

Q1. Match the following ROTI models with their descriptions:

1. Kirkpatrick Evaluation Model	A. Aligns training outcomes with organizational objectives across various perspectives including financial and learning.
2. The Bell System Approach	B. Built on Kirkpatrick's model, assesses reaction, capability, application, and worth outcomes.
3. Balanced Scorecard	C. Evaluates training at four levels: reactions, learning, behaviour, and results, with an additional level for ROI.

Q2. Match the following ROTI components with their definitions:

1. Training Costs	A. Tangible and intangible returns such as improved productivity and job satisfaction.
2. Training Benefits	B. Various expenses including course development, instructional materials, and travel.
3. ROTI Challenges	C. Subjective nature of benefits, delayed realization, and disruptions caused by data collection.

ANSWERS

CHAPTER 1: OVERCOMING PROCRASTINATION
Multiple Choice Type Questions
Answer 1. B   Answer 2. C   Answer 3. B   Answer 4. C

Answer 5. B

Match The Following
Answers 1.

1- C   2- A   3- B

CHAPTER 2: TIME MANAGEMENT
Multiple Choice Type Questions
Answer 1: B   Answer 2: C   Answer 3: C   Answer 4: B

Answer 5: B   Answer 6: B   Answer 7: C   Answer 8: A

Answer 9: D   Answer 10: C

Match The Following
Answers 1:

1 – B   2 – E   3 – A   4 – C   5 – D

CHAPTER 3: STRESS MANAGEMENT
Multiple Choice Type Questions
Answer 1: D   Answer 2: C   Answer 3: C   Answer 4: D

Answer 5: B   Answer 6: D   Answer 7: B   Answer 8: C

Match The Following
Answer 1:

1 – I   2 – G   3 – J   4 – A   5 – C   6 – B   7 – D   8 – E   9 – F   10 - H

Answer 2:

1 – D   2 - E   3 – A   4 – C   5 - B

CHAPTER 4: DEPRESSION MANAGEMENT

Multiple Choice Type Questions
Answer 1: C   Answer 2: B   Answer 3: C   Answer 4: D

Answer 5: A   Answer 6: B

Match The Following
Answers 1:

1- C   2- E   3 – D   4 – B   5 – A

CHAPTER 5: PRESENTATIONS SKILLS

Multiple Choice Type Question
Answer 1: B   Answer 2: B   Answer 3: B   Answer 4: C

Answer 5: C   Answer 6: B   Answer 7: C   Answer 8: B

Match The Following
Answer 1:

1 – D   2 – B   3 – A   4 – E   5 – G   6 – H   7 – C   8 - F

Answer 2:

1 – C   2 – B   3 - A

CHAPTER 6: SITUATIONAL AWARENESS

Multiple Choice Type Questions

Answer 1: B   Answer 2: D   Answer 3: C   Answer 4: B

Answer 5: A   Answer 6: D   Answer 7: D   Answer 8: D

Answer 9: B   Answer 10: B

Match The Following

Answer 1:

1 – B   2 – D   3 – A   4 - C

Answer 2:

1 – B   2 – A   3 – C   4 – D   5 - E

CHAPTER 7: COMMUNICATION PROFICIENCY

Multiple Choice Type Questions

Answer 1: D   Answer 2: C   Answer 3: B   Answer 4: C

Answer 5: B   Answer 6: C   Answer 7: D   Answer 8: C

Match The Following

Answer 1:

1 – B   2 – C   3 – D   4 - A

Answer 2:

1 – C   2 – D   3 – A   4 – B   5 - E

CHAPTER 8: MOTIVATION AT WORKPLACE

Multiple Choice Type Questions

Answer 1: C   Answer 2: C   Answer 3: B   Answer 4: B

Answer 5: D   Answer 6: A   Answer 7: B   Answer 8: B

Answer 9: B   Answer 10: B   Answer 11: C   Answer 12: B

Match The Following

Answers 1:

1- C   2- E   3- A   4- B   5- D

Answers 2.

1- B   2- A   3- E   4- D   5- C

CHAPTER 9: SIX THINKING HATS

Multiple Choice Type Questions

Answer 1: B   Answer 2: B   Answer 3: C   Answer 4: B

Answer 5: C   Answer 6: B   Answer 7: C   Answer 8: A

Answer 9: B   Answer 10: C

Match the Following

Answer 1:

1 – B   2 – C   3 – F   4 – A   5 – D   6 - E

CHAPTER 10: CREATIVITY AND ITS BLOCKS

Multiple Choice Type Questions

Answer 1: C   Answer 2: C   Answer 3: A   Answer 4: B

Answer 5: A   Answer 6: B   Answer 7: D   Answer 8: A

Answer 9: D   Answer 10: B   Answer 11: B   Answer 12: C

Answer 13: C   Answer 14: B   Answer 15: C   Answer 16: C

Match the Following

Answer 1:

1 – B   2 – F   3 – E   4 – A   5 – C   6 - D

Answer 2:

1 – B   2 – A   3 – D   4 – C   5 – E   6 - F

Answer 3:

1 – F   2 – D   3 – A   4 – B   5 – C   6 – E   7 - G

CHAPTER 11: CONFLICT MANAGEMENT

Multiple Choice Type Questions

Answer 1: A   Answer 2: C   Answer 3: C   Answer 4: C

Answer 5: C   Answer 6: A   Answer 7: C   Answer 8: C

Match the Following

Answer:

1 – B   2 - A   3 – D   4 – C   5 - E

CHAPTER 12: TEAM DYNAMICS

Multiple Choice Type Questions

Answer 1: A   Answer 2: D   Answer 3: B   Answer 4: B

Answer 5: B   Answer 6: C

Match the Following

Answer 1:

1 – H   2 – B   3 – A   4 – D   5 – C   6 – E   7 – F   8 - G

CHAPTER 13: TRANSACTIONAL ANALYSIS

Multiple Choice Type Questions

Answer 1: C   Answer 2: C   Answer 3: C   Answer 4: C

Answer 5: B   Answer 6: C   Answer 7: A   Answer 8: B

Match The Following

Answer 1:

1 – C   2 – F   3 – D   4 – A   5 – E   6 - B

CHAPTER 14: JOHARI'S WINDOW

Multiple Choice Type Questions

Answer 1: C   Answer 2: B   Answer 3: C   Answer 4: C

Answer 5: A   Answer 6: C

Match The Following
Answer 1:

1 - B   2 - D   3 – A   4 - C

CHAPTER 15: COMPETENCY MAPPING

Multiple Choice Type Questions

Answer 1: A   Answer 2: B   Answer 3: B   Answer 4: D

Answer 5: C   Answer 6: C   Answer 7: C   Answer 8: C

Match the Following
Answer 1:

1 – C   2 – A   3 – B   4 - D

Answer 2:

1 – C   2 – D   3 – A   4 - B

CHAPTER 16: LEADING AND MANAGING

Multiple Choice Type Questions

Answer 1: B   Answer 2: C   Answer 3: D   Answer 4: C

Answer 5: B   Answer 6: C   Answer 7: C   Answer 8: B

Match the Following
Answer 1:

1 – D   2 – B   3 – C   4 – E   5 - A

Answer 2

1 – C   2 – A   3 – B   4 – D   5 - E

CHAPTER 17: THEORY X AND THEORY Y

Multiple Choice Type Questions

Answer 1: B   Answer 2: B   Answer 3: B   Answer 4: B

Answer 5: B   Answer 6: D   Answer 7: B   Answer 8: A

Match The Following

Answer 1:

1- B   2- A

CHAPTER 18: POLARITY MANAGEMENT

Multiple Choice Type Questions

Answer 1: B   Answer 2: B   Answer 3: C   Answer 4: B

Answer 5: B   Answer 6: C

Match The Following

Answers 1:

1- D   2- C   3- B   4- A

CHAPTER 19: DECISION MAKING AND PROBLEM SOLVING

Multiple Choice Type Questions

Answer 1: B   Answer 2: B   Answer 3: C   Answer 4: C

Answer 5: C   Answer 6: D   Answer 7: B   Answer 8: C

Match the Following
Answer 1:

1 – E   2 – A   3 – B   4 – D   5 - C

Answer 2:

1 – D   2 – C   3 – B   4 – E   5 - A

CHAPTER 20: EFFECTIVENESS TO EXCELLENCE

Multiple Choice Type Questions
Answer 1: B   Answer 2: B   Answer 3: B   Answer 4: C

Answer 5: C   Answer 6: B   Answer 7: C   Answer 8: C

Match the Following
Answer 1:

1 – G   2 – E   3 – A   4 – B   5 – F   6 – C   7 – D

CHAPTER 21: RETURN ON TRAINING INVESTMENT

Multiple Choice Type Questions
Answer 1: B   Answer 2: C   Answer 3: B   Answer 4: C

Answer 5: C   Answer 6: B   Answer 7: D   Answer 8: B

Match the Following
Answer 1:

1 – C   2 – B   3 - A

Answer 2:

1 – B   2 – A   3 - C

BIBLIOGRAPHY

1. Eat That Frog! by Brian Tracy
2. The Now Habit by Neil A. Fiore
3. Solving the Procrastination Puzzle
4. Getting Things Done: The Art of Stress-Free Productivity by David Allen
5. The 7 Habits of Highly Effective People by Stephen R. Covey
6. Managing Workplace Stress: The Cognitive Behavioural Way by Dr. John Cooper and Dr. Lindsay Page
7. Stress Management for Life: A Research-Based Experiential Approach by Michael Olpin and Margie Hesson
8. Depression: A Public Feeling by Ann Cvetkovich
9. Managing Depression in Clinical Practice by Sagar V. Parikh
10. The Art of Public Speaking by Dale Carnegie
11. Presentation Zen: Simple Ideas on Presentation Design and Delivery by Garr Reynolds
12. You Can Influence People: A Non-Mechanical Approach to Public Speaking by Maheshwari
13. Principles of Personal Defense by Jeff Cooper
14. Boyd: The Fighter Pilot Who Changed the Art of War by Robert Coram
15. Situational Leadership: A Critical Review by Suresh C. Srivastva
16. Business Communication: Building Critical Skills by Kitty O. Locker and Raj K. Sharma
17. Nonverbal Communication in Human Interaction by Mark L. Knapp and Judith A. Hall
18. Communication Skills for Engineers and Scientists by Sangeeta Sharma
19. Organizational Behavior by Stephen P. Robbins and Timothy A. Judge
20. Managing Human Resources: People at Work by Luis R. Gomez-Mejia, David B. Balkin, and Robert L. Cardy

21. The Winning Way: Learnings from Sport for Managers by Anita Bhogle and Harsha Bhogle
22. Six Thinking Hats by Edward de Bono
23. Corporate Creativity by Pradip Khandwalla
24. The Five Dysfunctions of a Team: A Leadership Fable by Patrick Lencioni
25. Managing Conflict in Organizations by M. Afzalur Rahim
26. Understanding Organizational Behaviour by Udai Pareek and Sushama Khanna
27. Managing Teams: A Strategy for Success by Pradip N. Khandwalla
28. Transactional Analysis in Psychotherapy: A Systematic Individual and Social Psychiatry by Eric Berne
29. Johari's Window: A Model for Improving Interpersonal Communication and Leadership Effectiveness by Satish Pandey
30. Competency-Based Human Resource Management by S. K. Bhatia
31. Leadership: Theory and Practice by Peter G. Northouse
32. Primal Leadership: Unleashing the Power of Emotional Intelligence by Daniel Goleman, Richard Boyatzis, and Annie McKee
33. Excellence through Leadership: Learning from Indian Experiences by N. R. Narayana Murthy
34. The Human Side of Enterprise by Douglas McGregor
35. Organizational Behavior by Stephen P. Robbins and Timothy A. Judge
36. Polarity Management: Identifying and Managing Unsolvable Problems by Barry Johnson
37. Decision Making and Problem Solving Strategies by John Adair
38. Thinking, Fast and Slow by Daniel Kahneman
39. The 8th Habit: From Effectiveness to Greatness by Stephen R. Covey
40. The Training Measurement Book: Best Practices, Proven Methodologies, and Practical Approaches by Josh Bersin
41. Evaluating Training Programs: The Four Levels by Donald L. Kirkpatrick and James D. Kirkpatrick
42. Training and Development: A Comprehensive Approach by B. Janakiram and M. R. L. Narasimha Rao

ABOUT THE AUTHOR

Dr. Pranab Kumar Das Gupta is a distinguished professional with over 35 years of expertise in Computer Science and HR management. He currently holds the position of Associate Director and Senior Scientist at the Defence Research and Development Organisation (DRDO), India. Renowned for his leadership, training, and career guidance capabilities, he has significantly contributed to his field.

Dr. Das Gupta holds an M.Sc., M.Tech, and Ph.D. in Computer Science. He has furthered his professional development through executive training at prestigious institutions such as IIT Kharagpur, IIM Ahmedabad, IIM Kolkata and IIM Lucknow.

In addition to his technical accomplishments, Dr. Das Gupta is a committed educator and mentor, and has trained more than 2000 students. He is also an accomplished author, with 10 books and over 30 research papers to his credit. His motivational and interpersonal skills are augmented by his ability to impart values through the teachings, making him a sought-after consultant, educator, and career guide.

INDEX

www.ingramcontent.com/pod-product-compliance
Lightning Source LLC
Chambersburg PA
CBHW071917210526
45479CB00002B/445